PENGUIN BOOKS

MORBIDLY CURIOUS

Coltan Scrivner, PhD, is a behavioral scientist and horror entertainment producer. He is the world's leading expert on the science behind morbid curiosity and the appeal of frightening entertainment. He is also the executive director of the Nightmare in the Ozarks Film Festival and the Eureka Springs Zombie Crawl, one of the largest gatherings of zombies in the world.

Praise for MORBIDLY CURIOUS

"A fascinating examination of a feature of human nature that all of us have, most of us deplore (at least in others), and few of us understand." —**Steven Pinker,** *New York Times* **bestselling author of** *Rationality* **and** *Enlightenment Now*

"What sort of sickness drives our fascination with true crime, slasher films, and all things macabre? In this wonderfully unsettling exploration, Coltan Scrivner shows that morbid curiosity isn't a pathology at all—it's a form of preparation, one that deepens our empathy and builds our resilience. *Morbidly Curious* is sharp, humane, and a delight to read." —**Paul Bloom, author of** *Against Empathy* **and** *Psych*

"I can't look away from this book. Dr. Scrivner doesn't shy away from explaining some of the darkest recesses of our curious mind, and as a result we learn so much more about humans." —**Scott Barry Kaufman, author of** *Wired to Create* **and** *Transcend*

"An exhilarating and wise exploration. Through lively storytelling and fresh research, Scrivner illustrates how safely engaging with frightening experiences better prepares us for actual dangers. From predator detection in animals to the human fascination with horror films, morbid curiosity is revealed as a vital, evolved tool for survival." —**Rob Henderson, bestselling author of** *Troubled*

"A riveting exploration of our deepest, darkest fascinations. Once you start reading, you won't be able to look away." —**Steve Stewart-Williams, author of** *The Ape That Understood the Universe*

"*Morbidly Curious* is like a guided tour through a haunted mansion—a carefully crafted expedition with an expert guide to unveil the psychology behind the sinister and the spooky. Coltan Scrivner has a gift for extracting deep insights from our darker compulsions." —**Tania Lombrozo, director of the Concepts and Cognition Lab at Princeton University**

"*Morbidly Curious* is a smart, surprising, and even uplifting look at why we're drawn to true crime and horror. Scrivner uses cutting-edge science to show that our fascination with fear isn't something to hide from—it's a powerful instinct that keeps us safe and makes us human." —**Kurt Gray, author of *Outraged***

"Why are humans so captivated by blood and gore? In this razor-sharp book, Coltan Scrivner explains why our morbid curiosity is nothing to be ashamed of: It's a survival strategy honed by millions of years of natural selection. Combining cutting-edge science with mastery of pop culture, *Morbidly Curious* is a paean to the horror genre—and a window into human nature." —**David Pinsof, evolutionary psychologist and cocreator of Cards Against Humanity**

"The title piqued my curiosity. As I read, I became morbidly curious. By the end, I had a great time. In *Morbidly Curious*, Coltan Scrivner takes us on a fascinating journey through horror films, true crime, haunted houses, and psychological experiments, revealing how engaging with fear can be a form of play that eases anxiety and even makes us better people. A fun, stimulating, and enlightening read!" —**Daniel T. Blumstein, author of *The Nature of Fear***

"A remarkable journey that delves into why humans can't seem to look away from the things that some would refer to as unhealthy, shocking, or fearsome. . . . A must read for those who can't help looking at the scene of an accident, gazing cautiously at a menacing-looking animal hiding behind a bush, watching horror movies or combat sports with unfiltered fixation, or cautiously walking through a dark house to find the source of a random sound. . . . Refreshing." —***Library Journal* (starred review)**

"Scrivner blends research, analysis, folk tales, and pop culture to create a fascinating portrait of the human mind: why we seek the darkness, and what we can learn from it." —***Lit Hub***

MORBIDLY CURIOUS

A Scientist Explains
Why We Can't Look Away

COLTAN SCRIVNER, PHD

PENGUIN BOOKS

PENGUIN BOOKS
An imprint of Penguin Random House LLC
1745 Broadway, New York, NY 10019
penguinrandomhouse.com

Page 32: Photo by Keith Roper.
Page 41: Photo courtesy of South Tyrol Museum of
Archaeology/Samadelli/Staschitz—www.iceman.it.
Page 198: Photo courtesy of Marie Søndergaard.
Page 215: Photo courtesy of the Games for Emotional
and Mental Health Lab.

Set in Adobe Caslon Pro
Designed by Christina Nguyen

LIBRARY OF CONGRESS CATALOGING-IN-PUBLICATION DATA
Names: Scrivner, Coltan author
Title: Morbidly curious: a scientist explains why we can't
look away / Coltan Scrivner, PhD.
Description: New York, NY: Penguin Books, [2025] |
Includes bibliographical references and index.
Identifiers: LCCN 2025412026 (print) | LCCN 2025002351 (ebook) |
ISBN 9780143137344 trade paperback | ISBN 9780593511299 ebook
Subjects: LCSH: Death—Psychological aspects | Horror | Horror films—Appreciation
Classification: LCC BF789.D4 S37 2025 (print) |
LCC BF789.D4 (ebook) | DDC 155.9/37—dc23/eng/20250702
LC record available at https://lccn.loc.gov/2025412026
LC ebook record available at https://lccn.loc.gov/2025002351

Printed in the United States of America
2nd Printing

The authorized representative in the EU for product safety and compliance is
Penguin Random House Ireland, Morrison Chambers, 32 Nassau Street,
Dublin D02 YH68, Ireland, https://eu-contact.penguin.ie.

To those with dark minds, but soft hearts.

CONTENTS

MORBIDLY
CURIOUS

PROLOGUE

In 2004, *Saw* brought the gore/splatter subgenre of horror into the mainstream. Nearly twenty years, eight films, and over one billion dollars later, *Saw* has become one of the most popular horror franchises of all time. The films center around a serial killer vigilante named Jigsaw who kidnaps and tortures people, subjecting them to physical or psychological torment he calls "games" in order to test their will to survive—and to pay for their ungratefulness in life.

When *Spiral*, the ninth installment in the franchise, came out in 2021, it received a blistering review from *New York Post* movie critic Johnny Oleksinski. Fans of *Saw*, Oleksinski wrote, are "depraved lunatics who should not be allowed near animals or most other living things." He goes on in his review to say that "these so-called movies are completely and utterly worthless and barely deserve to exist on the periphery of cinema."

Ouch.

I've never encountered a critique quite as vitriolic as this *Spiral* review. It wasn't just the film that got trashed in the review; the fans were dragged down with it. According to Oleksinski, enjoying the *Saw* films wasn't just a matter of taste or class. Instead, it was a matter of moral standing. Someone who enjoys the depiction of gruesome violence must also find violence acceptable in real life. Applying this logic, fans of movies like *Saw* must be dangerous.

Oleksinski's moral outrage isn't new. Critics throughout cinematic history have written about the supposedly depraved nature of horror fans, but no decade saw more panic around horror movies than the 1980s. The decade began with a machete-wielding masked killer stalking teens at Camp Crystal Lake. *Friday the 13th* was a success at the box office, drawing in nearly sixty million dollars worldwide. Despite its success, the film was not as widely embraced by critics as its thrilling older brother, *Halloween* (1978). *Friday the 13th* was much bloodier, and critics took note.

Renowned film critic Gene Siskel was one of the most outspoken critics of slashers generally, and *Friday the 13th* specifically. In his review of *Friday the 13th*, Siskel levied the heaviest punishment possible by a critic: He intentionally spoiled the ending to dissuade people from watching. And if that weren't enough, he concluded his review by publishing the name and address of Paramount chairman Charles Bluhdorn, encouraging readers to send him hate mail. He tried to do the same for starring actress Betsy Palmer, but he was unable to find her private address, so he encouraged readers to mail their complaints to her small hometown of Rowayton, Connecticut.

In addition to his column in the *Chicago Tribune*, Siskel cohosted a television show called *Sneak Previews* with the legendary film critic Roger Ebert. Neither critic was a fan of slasher movies, and the duo decided to dedicate an entire episode of their show to rebuking *Friday the 13th* and the spate of slashers that had cropped up after the success of *Halloween*. Siskel's palpable ire for the film bled into outrage at its fans, much like in Oleksinski's review of *Spiral*. Siskel speculated that fans of *Friday the 13th* were "some very sick people" who "hate women."

Rather than confirming that they're sick people who hate women, my research shows that fans of slashers and other horror movies are simply morbidly curious. Morbid curiosity is a straightforward concept: When the costs of learning about a threat are low, it's advantageous to pay attention and gather information. In these times, we feel curious—morbidly curious. It's a remarkably simple idea, but it is influenced by a complex array of experiences and traits, and it manifests in myriad ways.

It's worth clarifying here what I mean by "morbidly curious." It's a phrase that can be easily misunderstood. I don't mean that the curiosity itself is morbid. When I say morbid curiosity, I am not referring to a pathological, abnormal, or unhealthy curiosity. The descriptor "morbid" here is simply referring to death or the things that lead to it; morbid curiosity is a curiosity about things that are threatening or potentially dangerous. In my research, I've discovered that morbid curiosity tends to fall into four categories: (1) minds of dangerous people, (2) physical violence, (3) bodily injuries, and (4) paranormal dangers. I've also developed the Morbid Curiosity Scale, which scientists use to assess how morbidly curious a person is and where they fall with respect to these four categories. As we'll see throughout this book, your level of morbid curiosity is a powerful predictor of certain behaviors and can even positively influence your psychological well-being.

Given that there are four broad categories of morbid curiosity, there are many different ways one might engage in morbidly curious behavior. For example, watching horror movies is a common everyday example of morbid curiosity in modern times. Themes in horror movies span the spectrum of morbid curiosity, from paranormal threats to serial killers and outlandish bodily injuries. However, not every morbidly curious person is a horror fan (though every horror fan is likely more morbidly curious than the average person). Because horror fandom maps quite well on to all four categories of morbid curiosity, there will be several times throughout the book where I'll talk about the psychology of horror fans as a core group representing people who are morbidly curious. This will be a familiar shorthand to many of you; horror movies, books, and spooky cultural artifacts are all around us.

Not everyone has a strong impulse toward morbid curiosity. Why, then, are some of us so powerfully drawn to content that portrays evil, violence, and suffering? Is an interest in the darker side of life a sign of moral bankruptcy? In my experience, this isn't an accurate assessment. I've met with and studied morbidly curious people all over the world, from haunted attractions to horror conventions to university classrooms. Anecdotally and empirically, morbidly curious people are just as moral, empathetic, and kind as anyone else. If you attend a horror convention or an oddities expo, you won't run into deranged psychopaths waiting to catch you alone in a dark hallway. Instead, you'll find a genuine community of people with skin thickened from years of side-eyes and hushed comments. You'll find people with dark minds but soft hearts.

This book is filled with the latest research on the science of morbid curiosity. As a pioneer of psychological research on this topic, much of the research I talk about will be studies that I led or was involved in. Since several of these studies were published in just the past few years, I expect a lot of this information to be new to many readers. After an overview of what morbid curiosity is in chapter 1, I'll explore its origins in life on Earth throughout chapter 2. You'll come to find that the roots of morbid curiosity are much older than we may think and that some form of it is found in many animals. If zebras could watch movies about lions stalking their prey, they probably would. In the next few chapters, I'll dive into the details of my new theory of why we seek out the macabre through true crime, ghost stories, violent entertainment, gruesome art, and other cultural artifacts.

In chapter 7, we'll take a detour through the dream world and examine a question that people have been asking for millennia: What are dreams for? Chapter 8 will have you questioning what you thought you knew about empathy. As it turns out, enjoying a film where teens get slashed by a masked killer may not be a sign of low empathy. Chapters 9 and 10 will explain why we seek out scary media when the world is scary and how this might help us become more resilient. Rather than escape from a scary world into happy, safe fictions, we often escape into fictional worlds even more terrifying than our own. You'll also learn about the psychological benefits of morbid curiosity through stories of scientific expeditions at haunted attractions. In news that may not come as a surprise to parents, chapter 11 will explore why kids are so drawn to evil villains and scary play and why exploring these concepts through play can be good for their children's psychological development.

Despite how vital it is to human nature, morbid curiosity has historically been maligned and unfairly vilified. Those with an overt interest in the macabre are sometimes seen as problematic and cast as outsiders. My central argument in this book is that this negative view of morbid curiosity is mistaken. Far from being a stain on our psyche, my research shows that morbid curiosity is a common and healthy aspect of our psychology. It's a relic of our evolutionary history that can continue to serve us in the modern world.

For the morbidly curious readers, I hope you'll find some insight about yourself as you read: why you love true crime, despite feeling disgust toward the killer; why Halloween gives you a cozy feeling; and why you sometimes just can't look away. For those without a penchant for the macabre, you'll come to understand your friend who can't stop talking about the latest horror movie or whose dream car is an old hearse.

The academics who pick up this book will find a fresh and more complete explanation of a topic that feels familiar but has yet to be thoroughly explored. Behavioral ecologists will be familiar with the work on predator inspection that I discuss but see it applied to humans in a new and fascinating way; anthropologists may recognize stories from the Ecuadorian Shuar, the West African Beng, and the Mehinaku of central Brazil but see those stories woven together with new research on anxiety, fear, and curiosity; psychologists will recognize some of the research on threat detection but find their results being explained from a different framework. The interdisciplinary nature of this project on morbid curiosity draws on empirical findings and theoretical frameworks from many different domains, making it relevant for a wide range of scholars.

The science of morbid curiosity is just beginning to blossom. The following pages will explain our attraction to the macabre and explore the evolutionary origins of morbid curiosity, its role in shaping what entertainment we seek out, how it relates to other personality traits, and its surprising effects on our mental health and well-being. We'll also explore some contentious questions: Does morbid curiosity cause psychopaths to kill? Can empathy lead us morally astray? Should you let your kids engage in scary play? The pages of this book will cover some of the darkest crevices of the human psyche—and, perhaps, scratch a morbidly curious itch along the way.

1.

WHY WE CAN'T LOOK AWAY

Out of this nettle, danger,
we pluck this flower, safety.

—William Shakespeare

A DARK PAST

Room 218. Here it was. I stood outside the door for several minutes, fiddling with the key and jiggling the doorknob, trying to get the lock to budge. Jokingly, I mumbled, "Okay, Michael, I'm just trying to get into my room—I mean, *your* room." The lock immediately clicked, and the door creaked open. The room was empty. I stepped inside and looked around. There didn't seem to be anything special about the room; a TV sat atop an old dresser with a king-size bed positioned across from it. In front of me was a door that opened to a veranda overlooking the Ozark Mountains. Room 218 looked pretty much like every other room on the second floor. But something felt off.

The Crescent Hotel in Eureka Springs, Arkansas, bills itself as America's Most Haunted Hotel. Built in 1886 atop a hill in the

Ozark Mountains, the Crescent has a dark, specter-ridden history. Some of the more commonly sighted ghosts include a child named Breckie who wanders the halls at night, a nameless woman who falls from the top floor of the hotel, Dr. Ellis and his cherry-flavored pipe, and Morris, the old, orange hotel cat. However, it was Michael, the first ghost to inhabit the Crescent, who I was here to see.

According to legend, Michael was a young Irish stonemason and a member of the crew that built the Crescent Hotel. Not much is known about him, but the stories always mention his flirtatious nature. While working atop the Crescent one day, Michael spotted a beautiful woman walking by. Not one to pass on a chance to meet a lovely woman, he leaned over the edge of a beam and shouted to catch her attention. Unfortunately, he leaned a little too far and lost his balance. Michael fell from the top of the Crescent's skeletal structure and landed on a support beam in the wall of what is now room 218.

The Crescent Hotel, circa 1890s.

Michael's fall was only the first in a string of mysterious and unfortunate deaths at the Crescent. In the 1930s a con man named Norman Baker bought the Crescent and turned it into a sham cancer hospital. Baker's "Cancer Curable Hospital," as he called it, offered a miracle cure, a secret "Formula 5," that was injected into tumors. Dozens of patients died in the Crescent during Baker's time at its helm. Patients would grow sicker by the day as their cancer went untreated. When their screams of pain began to fill the halls, they were moved to the psychiatric ward. Of course there were no actual psychiatrists on staff.

The psychiatric ward was an isolated wing of the Crescent where the loudest patients were free to scream. After succumbing to the infernal combination of untreated cancer and Baker's bogus injections, deceased patients were quietly shuttled to the basement morgue before being cremated in the dead of night. As far as the other patients knew, those who were not around anymore had been cured and sent home—not released through the crematory chimney.

A number of hotel rooms now occupy the wing of the Crescent that used to house the so-called psychiatric patients. Guests often report foul smells emanating from the walls of these rooms. Ghostly sightings are also common in this part of the hotel. Some guests describe seeing a nurse pushing a gurney down the hallway, only to disappear into thin air. Others report hearing terrible sounds throughout the night, such as the screech of unoiled wheels on the hallway floors and haunting screams of pain.

A good night's sleep isn't usually in the cards for those who stay in the more paranormally active rooms. Rumor has it that Michael's poltergeist likes to play tricks on guests who stay in room 218. Many report feeling as if someone touched them—a flick of the hair or a stroke on their arm—despite lying in bed alone. Others say they've experienced the shower quickly change from hot to cold and back to hot again.

I spent one night in Michael's room. I didn't feel any strange presence while lying in bed, nor did I have any issues with the shower temperature. But I did experience something else that I can't quite explain. I was watching television late at night when I saw a dresser drawer slowly creep open in front of me, as if someone was carefully pulling it out. I got up to shut the drawer more than once that night.

According to the staff at the Crescent, Michael's room is the most paranormally active in the hotel. It's also the most requested, with the other paranormally active rooms following closely behind. It's not uncommon for Michael's room to be booked several months in advance, with holidays and certain weekends sometimes reserved nearly a year out. The popularity doesn't come from the amenities, size, or view; you couldn't distinguish a photo of Michael's room from a photo of any other on the second floor of the hotel. The only thing that is special about Michael's room is Michael.

Unlike typical hotels, where the staff work diligently to ensure their guests get a restful night's sleep, the Crescent flaunts the disruptive ghosts of its past. There's an entire website dedicated to spooky activities and experiences that visitors can purchase during their stay. Guests who don't believe in ghosts are often intrigued enough to book a night in one of the haunted rooms; I was one of them!

So why is this? Why would anyone want to stay at a supposedly haunted hotel and spend extra money for the most haunted room in the entire place?

Haunted rooms are popular for the same reason the Romans gathered by the thousands in the Colosseum, why true crime has taken over television and podcasts, and why we find ourselves staring at a car wreck on the side of the road. These things derive their popularity from our morbid curiosity.

DRAWN TO THE DARK SIDE

We have all experienced morbid curiosity at one point or another. It's that peculiar feeling of fascination that motivates us to face fear, disgust, and the unknown. It's the ambivalence we feel when presented with a sight that is disgusting yet mysteriously alluring. It's the hesitation we experience just before entering a haunted house on Halloween, our bodies trembling and our minds stirring with a cocktail of excitement and fear. Horrific events, terrifying stories, and scary play hijack our attention and seduce our imagination. When something bad happens in the world, we want to be the first to hear about it. We can imagine terrible events with ease. Sometimes we even have to fight against the urge to conjure up unfortunate events. We have to convince ourselves not to think about the plane malfunctioning and crashing when there's a bit of turbulence and the seat belt light flashes on.

Psychologists have long argued that humans possess a negativity bias, or a tendency to be more affected by negative events than by positive ones. Negative events capture our attention faster, increase our arousal more, provoke stronger responses, and are remembered with ease compared to positive or neutral events. The pit in your stomach you get from losing a thousand dollars is a lot stronger than the elation that arises after winning a thousand dollars. A nasty breakup is more memorable than an amicable one. Negative feedback packs a stronger punch than positive feedback. In short, emotions, interactions, events, and situations perceived as "bad" impact us more strongly. We feel them more strongly, process the information related to them more thoroughly, and remember them more vividly. As social psychologist Roy Baumeister has said, bad is stronger than good.

But what does it mean for something to be negative or bad? These are very general terms. Of course, you know a negative event when you experience it. Losing a loved one, failing an exam, going through a rough breakup, suffering an injury—almost everyone would agree that these are negative experiences. However, science can't work with "you know it when you see it." Even something like violence, which seems like it would be clearly categorized as bad, is not so straightforward. The violence perpetrated by a bully on an innocent victim will likely be perceived as bad, but the violence enacted upon a villain by a noble hero likely will not. Negativity is subjective and can change depending on the context and the person experiencing it.

We've all heard that bad news travels faster than good news. It's something that is often chalked up to our negativity bias. But as cognitive anthropologist Pascal Boyer has shown, it's really *threatening* news that travels the fastest. Boyer has argued that our negativity bias is driven by threat-related information specifically, rather than negative information more generally.

Threat-related information is seen as more important than other kinds of information, and people who spread threatening information are seen as more reliable and trustworthy. Consider news anchors: Each day, they mostly share information about murders, thefts, and disasters. To them and their viewers, these topics are seen as more important than most other news. Despite the doom and gloom, many anchors who spread threatening information on a daily basis are popular and well respected by their viewers.

Boyer and his colleague Timothy Blaine demonstrated this principle empirically in a clever set of studies where they gave participants a list of facts about a product and asked them to pass on some of that information to a friend who was thinking of buying the product. Each report contained two negative statements, two threat-related statements, and four neutral statements. For example, one product was a one-step hair dye. Participants were asked to choose which statements from the following they would pass on to a friend who was thinking of buying the product. However, they could choose only seven of the eight. Which statement would you leave out?

- Flash Ultra Color™ may burn or irritate the scalp if applied to certain skin types.

- Flash Ultra Color™ can cause severe allergic reactions.

- Flash Ultra Color™ may fade in just a few days.

- Flash Ultra Color™ cannot be returned after being opened.

- Flash Ultra Color™ transforms naturally dark hair into super reflective tones.

- Flash Ultra Color™ includes premium grapeseed oils in its hair color formula.

- Flash Ultra Color™ spreads easily when applied and has a no-drip guarantee.

- Flash Ultra Color™ provides an online color selection tool to find your preferred shade.

The seven statements that were chosen were then passed on to a new participant, who would choose six of the seven to pass on to a new participant, who would choose five of the six, and so forth until only one statement remained. Negative statements (e.g., may fade in a few days) did make it to the end more often than neutral statements (e.g., includes premium grapeseed oils in its hair color formula), in line with previous studies on negativity bias. However, statements with threat-related information (e.g., can cause severe allergic reactions) were much more likely to make it to the end of the transmission chain than negative statements. In other words, participants saw the statements that contained information about danger as the most important information to spread to others.

We even have threat-related biases for threats that are unlikely to occur. In a follow-up study, Boyer showed that the likelihood of the threat transpiring had very little impact on how important the information was perceived to be. Even if the chance of the hair dye burning or irritating the scalp was 2 percent, participants were much more likely to pass this information on to another person.

Our sensitivity to threat-related information can be explained in part by something called the smoke detector principle. It's far better for the smoke detector in your house to trigger falsely when you accidentally overcook your dinner than for it to not trigger when there is an actual fire. The smoke detector is built to be sensitive to danger. Because of this, false positives occur more often, meaning you occasionally have to deal with a loud beeping when you are cooking despite there not being a fire.

When it comes to actual smoke detectors, these false positives are usually nothing more than minor annoyances or inconveniences; you have to endure a few seconds of obnoxious beeping every now and then. The same principle is generally true of the mind. It's better to be too vigilant than not vigilant enough. It's safer for you to be curious about what caused that rustling in the bushes than ignore it. It doesn't cost too much energy for your body to prepare itself for a potential danger lurking in the bushes, and there's a huge payoff if something is really there. Of course, you can overdo it. If the sensitivity is turned up too much, it will respond too often to even the smallest indications of danger, which can lead to pathological anxiety.

Responding half a second faster to potential danger won't determine your fate 99 percent of the time. But that 1 percent of the time that it does can be life or death. Psychologists John Tierney and Roy Baumeister summed this up nicely in their book *The Power of Bad*: "To survive, life has to win every day. Death has to win only once."

Over time, animals that responded more quickly to threats had a slight advantage in escaping. Scale this up to the population level, to millions of individuals over millions of years, and you'll see a shift in the average response time to threat across a population of individuals: natural selection in action. Animals, including humans, have slowly evolved to become more and more sensitive to and curious about threats in their environment. The consequence of millions of years of slight successes for those with predispositions to attend to and seek out information about potential threats has left its imprint on our psychology. This imprint also lies at the core of our morbid curiosity.

PREDATOR PREPARATION

Threats can come in many shapes and sizes, but the main danger that most animals face is predation. A quick and effective reaction to a potential predator is one of the most important traits an animal can have. Rather than having a key species that hunts them, like a cheetah to a gazelle, humans have faced terrifying new predators throughout their migration across the globe. Because of this, it's beneficial for us to quickly learn whether or not an animal might be dangerous.

If I ask you to imagine a predator, what features come to mind? You are probably imagining it to have large teeth, sharp claws, and a considerable size. These are all common features of mammalian predators. It is easy to see why this is the case. Being large and having big teeth and claws helps you capture, overpower, and consume your prey. The ubiquity of these features in predators makes it easier for us to identify potentially dangerous animals. We don't have to know much about an animal before we are able to recognize that it might be a bad idea to meet one in the wild. The universal threat of predation from large carnivores has left its mark on human psychology.

Having a predisposition to quickly identify and more easily remember information about dangerous animals gives a species a significant advantage in the evolutionary long run. In the scientific literature, this predisposition is called prepared learning.

Studies that investigate prepared learning often involve children or juveniles of a species since they are less likely to have encountered specific objects or situations in the environment. The idea is to see how animals respond to a particular stimulus without prior exposure to it. Language and culture make this a tricky topic to study in humans. Even if a small child has never personally experienced something, they may have seen it on TV, read it in a book, or heard about it from a friend or family member. Still, creative scientists have found ways to study prepared learning in children.

In a study that included American children in Los Angeles and Shuar children in Ecuador, anthropologist H. Clark Barrett and his colleagues tested prepared learning about dangerous animals. Their hypothesis was that children would be better at learning whether an animal was dangerous than they would be at remembering if the animal ate plants or animals.

After just a single training session, the evidence for prepared learning about danger was evident: US children correctly answered over 70 percent of the questions about danger and Shuar children correctly answered nearly 90 percent—a massive increase compared to no training. The effect of training on remembering diet was much smaller in the Shuar (63 percent correct) and virtually nonexistent in US children (52 percent correct). When the children were given the same test a week later, the results looked nearly identical, with information about danger being recalled correctly much more often than information about diet.

The children's minds were prepared to learn about danger. The same morbidly curious tendencies that saved generations of their ancestors could be seen in the results of a modern-day psychology study. The human mind evolved to be prepared to learn about threats, and this impacts how we interact with the world today, even in the absence of real predators.

THE SOLUTION TO THE PROBLEM OF DANGER

To effectively avoid and deal with threats, we need to learn about them. This means that our inclination to be repulsed by or afraid of dangerous situations must be counterbalanced by curiosity. We need to collect information about what a dangerous animal or person is like, how it behaves, and what the consequences of interacting with it might be. The result is two opposing motivations: one to approach the potential danger, and another to avoid it.

Our minds compare the costs and benefits of a given interaction to determine which of these competing motivations to heed. The potential to learn something useful or feel the exhilaration and excitement of danger's proximity entices us. At the same time, we want to avoid injury and the disgust, shame, or sadness that might accompany interacting with danger. While this cost-benefit calculation may sometimes bubble up to the level of conscious awareness, it's often something that occurs in the subconscious parts of our mind, guiding our behaviors without conscious intrusion.

We all measure the benefits and costs of threats differently. You may need more benefits than someone else in order to indulge in your morbid curiosity. Or maybe you're less bothered by disgust, so threat-related information that involves disgust doesn't bother you as much. Maybe you live in a dangerous area or perceive the world to be dangerous, so the benefits of learning threat-related information are more important for your survival.

The factors that influence the weight of the cost and the benefits are complex and multifaceted, but the basic computation is the same. This calculation exists in nearly all animals, but as we'll see later in the book, the human form of morbid curiosity is increasingly complex and interesting because humans can *imagine* situations. Imagining dangerous situations allows humans to drastically reduce the costs of engaging with threat-related information, making humans the most morbidly curious creatures around.

By their very nature, dangerous situations hold valuable information, especially if the situation is uncommon. When you find yourself in a rare or surprising situation, you might feel a sense of urgency about it. If you pass a wreck on the road and see a body lying on a stretcher, you may feel compelled to look. Some thoughts about the situation might even pass through your mind. "Is that guy dead? I'm not sure that I've ever seen a corpse. Who knows the next time I'll see a dead body. I'd better get a look at this one. . . ."

Sometimes the cost of gathering threat-related information is high, putting us at danger of physical injury or death. If I am a victim of a robbery, I do learn something about danger. But the threat to my physical safety far outweighs any learning benefit. Or let's say I witness someone else being robbed. Here again, I'm learning something about violence, but I'm still in danger of being injured and have a competing motivation to help the person being robbed. Because of the high costs of these situations, we typically don't seek them out. This is the way most animals learn about danger; they are either victims to it or witness another animal being subjected to it.

This leads to lower levels of morbidly curious behavior in most animals.

Humans have clever ways of driving down the cost of witnessing danger and learning about it. Technology allows us to experience robberies without any of the danger attached, fueling our morbid curiosity. This is why security camera footage of a robbery reliably draws viewers on the evening news. Humans even take this a step further and create stories of robberies that never transpired. With a story, there's no real risk of injury or death to the audience. This combination of low costs while retaining learning benefits stokes the fires of our morbid curiosity.

TELLING SCARY STORIES

Although we like to think of ourselves as being at the top of the food chain, humans have been preyed upon by a variety of creatures throughout history. We have managed to codify these predators in our folklore, with local species appearing in nearly every culture's tales. The stories involving these local predators use engaging narratives to explain how the predator behaves, what it eats, where it lives, and other information that one would want to know before encountering the animal in the wild. In other words, these stories are not just for entertainment; they also communicate important information about the dangers someone may encounter.

One story about a predator that many of you are probably familiar with is the tale of Little Red Riding Hood and the Big Bad Wolf. Although we probably won't find ourselves talking to a wolf pretending to be an old woman, "Little Red Riding Hood" does contain some elements of truth about wolves. These nuggets of information are embedded within an entertaining narrative, making it the perfect way to teach young children about a dangerous predator.

Let's think back to some of the key lines in the tale:

> "Grandmother, what big arms you have!"
> "All the better to hug you with, my dear."
> "Grandmother, what big legs you have!"
> "All the better to run with, my child."
> "Grandmother, what big ears you have!"
> "All the better to hear with, my child."
> "Grandmother, what big eyes you have!"
> "All the better to see with, my child."
> "Grandmother, what big teeth you have got!"
> "All the better to eat you up with."

Here, the young audience learns what wolves look like: They have large legs, large ears, large eyes, and large teeth. The story also tells the reader what these parts of the animal are for: Wolves use their big forelimbs to grasp their prey; they have strong hind legs that allow them to quickly chase down their meals; excellent hearing and large eyes allow them to locate animals from a distance; their big teeth will prove fatal if they catch you. The story also takes place in the woods, where you'd be most likely to encounter a wolf. Even the main character is constructed to be relatable to the intended audience. Little Red Riding Hood herself is a naïve child: exactly the kind of person who is likely to fall prey to a wolf.

Wolves are not an animal you tend to see walking about when you are a child. And, if you do see one, you might not live to tell the tale. In fact, the closest thing to a wolf that a child might see is its domesticated cousin. Unless told otherwise, children who grew up with dogs in prehistory might have thought wolves were perfectly friendly animals.

Sometimes the predators in our stories are not ripped straight from the natural world. Instead of a story about a wolf, we may tell the story of a werewolf, which is larger, more dangerous, and more frightening. Much like real predators, monsters in our stories lurk about in the shadows. The typical monster is a large-bodied beast with sharp teeth, long claws, formidable strength, and a bad temper. Sound familiar? Think of our most notorious horror monsters: What do they all have in common?

> Dracula has oversize canine teeth and, in some depictions, sharp claws.
>
> Werewolves have large claws and a mouth full of terrifying teeth.
>
> Michael Myers chases his victims with a menacing knife.
>
> Jason Voorhees wields a machete.
>
> Pennywise has a huge mouth full of knifelike teeth.
>
> Freddy Krueger wears a razor-claw glove.

Most monsters either possess sharp natural weaponry, like teeth or claws, or they wield sharp weapons that function like those biological features. The dangerous features of monsters mimic the dangerous features of natural predators. In fact, it's difficult to think of *any* popular horror monster that doesn't follow this rule, even when there are more effective means of violence. A machete isn't the best weapon if you are trying to kill a bunch of teenagers at a summer camp. A chain saw might sound scary, but it's heavy and requires gas to function. Neither of these is the best tool for the killer's job—that is, unless the killer's job is to terrify. These large, sharp weapons claw deep into our minds, activating evolutionarily old neural circuits for evading predators.

Good horror writers understand this connection. Wes Craven, who created the infamous horror monster Freddy Krueger, said that he gave Freddy a razor-claw glove because he was "looking for a primal fear that is embedded in the subconscious of all people of all cultures." One of those primal fears, he thought, was the claws of a predator. The claw glove isn't particularly lethal—killing a victim requires Freddy to be up close, often requires more than one slash, and involves a lot of chasing. However, those big claws trigger deeply rooted fears. Likewise, being chased triggers areas of the brain that evolved to help us escape predators. This is why stalking and chase scenes work so well in horror movies. Running around with a loud, rumbling chain saw that requires fuel to function is a terrible tactic if you want to efficiently kill someone. But it is one of the best ways to arouse fear and prompt antipredation behaviors.

Morbid curiosity is nature's way of putting us into situations where we can safely learn about the dangers of the world and how we respond in times of fear and anxiety. Sometimes this happens opportunistically—when we pass a car wreck, see a street fight break out, or catch a homicide story as we flip through the news. Other times, we seek out information about danger. We tell scary stories, watch horror movies, read about disasters, visit haunted locations, listen to true crime podcasts, spread threatening rumors, and play with fear in all kinds of ways. Morbid curiosity sits at the core of human nature and is infused in our cultures. Our species would be unrecognizable without it.

2.

THE EVOLUTION OF A
MORBIDLY CURIOUS CREATURE

As soon as there is life, there is danger.

—*Germaine de Staël*

PREDATOR AND PREY

Annie arrived late one morning to her favorite brunch spot, a place she had frequented with friends for years. It was upscale with plenty of vegan options and outdoor space to enjoy the sun. Annie loved it there and often spent hours savoring her meal with friends. In fact, the only thing she didn't like about this spot was Leon. A notorious local trouble-maker, Leon would loiter near Annie and her friends during their Sunday brunch gatherings. He would sit alone and watch the other diners without engaging with anyone. Annie, suspicious of his motives, kept a vigilant eye on him. Leon never seemed to be eating, and he never had any company. Annie couldn't fathom why he would come at all.

Something felt different this morning. Leon fixated intensely on one of Annie's friends as she ate her brunch. He began circling the area, slowly closing in on their location. Annie's friend didn't seem to notice him, but Annie, transfixed by the unfolding scene, felt a surge of adrenaline. Sensing danger, she let out a yelp and the girls bolted, leaving their brunch behind. Leon, abandoning stealth, gave chase. He was out to get one of them, but thanks to Annie's intuition and keen observation, she and her friends managed to escape.

This is a story about a typical interaction between an antelope and a lion on the savanna, though you could be forgiven for mistaking it for a scene in a thriller movie. Interactions between predators and prey, hunter and hunted, share several similarities across the animal kingdom. This dynamic has existed for millions of years; predators need to eat prey to stay alive, and prey need to avoid predators to stay alive. This is true from the microscopic level to the megafauna level, with predators and prey forever locked in a zero-sum game, evolving new features to outmaneuver each other. Sometimes these adaptations can be quite straightforward, like stronger legs for bursts of speed or larger claws for capturing prey. Other times, they can be spectacular, like the long quills of a porcupine or the 650-volt charge of the electric eel.

As we'll see, our human penchant for morbid curiosity is a product of nature's enduring struggle. To understand its origins, we must journey far back in time, to the muddy waters of the Cambrian Period.

AN EYE FOR DANGER

A critical development to come out of this ongoing battle between predators and prey was the evolution of the eye. Believe it or not, there was a time in Earth's history when organisms lacked the ability to see. Eyes simply did not exist, and organisms made their way through the dark world—at this time, a dark, watery world—using rudimentary versions of other senses. Eventually, random mutations in certain genes led a few cells on the outer layer of the skin to become sensitive to photons of light. It may have taken millions of years for the right mutations to align, but when they did, it gave rise to a new sense: a primitive form of sight. This sense was remarkably simple, providing only a vague ability to perceive shadows in the light from the waters above. However, it provided a crucial advantage when it came to escaping predators or capturing prey.

These initial eyespots triggered an evolutionary arms race. Zoologist Andrew Parker has put forth a convincing theory that the emergence of the eye led to the most significant surge in species proliferation and complexity the world has ever seen: the Cambrian Explosion. Once the "lights" were turned on, as Parker quips, species faced an adapt-or-die scenario. In just one million years, the world of organisms went from around three phyla (major taxonomic groups of living beings) to the over thirty phyla we see today. A million years may sound like a long time, but it's a mere speck on the evolutionary timeline. This remarkable transformation is so apparent in the fossil record that it even prompted Darwin to question his evolutionary thinking. How could so much complexity evolve in the blink of an evolutionary eye?

To maintain their advantage in the face of increasingly efficient predators, prey species evolved sensitive detection thresholds to perceive potential threats. By erring on the side of overdetection, prey may experience more false alarms but fewer missed detections—the smoke detector principle we saw in chapter 1. Across species and in numerous domains, overactive detection evolved as a way for animals to keep the edge in life's evolutionary race.

One example of overactive predator detection is the visual looming bias. In many species, rapidly approaching or expanding objects trigger defensive behaviors. Studies with humans show that approaching objects are estimated to be traveling faster than receding objects moving at the same speed. A similar bias exists with sound: We are more alert to sounds of approaching objects than receding ones. These slight cognitive biases give prey an important advantage when it comes to detecting predators. By overestimating the speed of an approaching threat, prey can react slightly faster, increasing the likelihood of escaping from a predator.

Of course, predator species adapt alongside prey species to counter these perceptual biases. Take lions, for example. Despite their formidable size and impressive speed, they have evolved into stealthy hunters. They strategically lurk in savanna grasses, looking to sneak up on their prey. Over hundreds of thousands of years of evolution, a lion's body gradually transformed into that of a premier stealth hunter. Soft footpads muffle the sound of carefully placed paws, tan fur blends in with the tall savanna grasses, and precise vision, acute hearing, and a strong sense of smell enable them to track prey from a distance. These seemingly minor adaptations add up to make the lion a more elusive hunter that can effectively evade the heightened senses of their prey.

PREDATOR INSPECTION

Although lions are expert hunters, they aren't always on the prowl for a meal. Sometimes, perhaps even most of the time, lions are neither hungry nor engaged in hunting. In fact, lions spend over twenty hours a day lounging around (a fact that may not be surprising to anyone who has a cat at home). It's in a lion's best interest to chase after a potential meal only when it's hungry. Hunting is energetically costly; those quick bursts of speed as lions leap out of their stealth burn tons of calories. Not to mention that they don't always successfully capture their prey. If the prey escapes, the hunting expedition becomes a costly caloric debt.

Even if a lion does manage to catch a zebra or a wildebeest, it needs to be hungry enough to consume it right away. There are no storage freezers on the savanna, and a dead animal will either be eaten right away by the predator that caught it or become fair game for a group of bold scavengers. Even hungry lions often have to fend off hyenas and other carnivores to keep their meal. Because of these constraints, lions and other predators typically engage in a hunt only when they are hungry. Remarkably, the prey animals of the savanna seem to know this.

Just as it's energetically wasteful for a lion to hunt when it isn't hungry, it's also inefficient for zebras or wildebeests to flee every time they spot a lion. Lions and their prey live in proximity, often within each other's line of sight. If prey animals were to bolt each time they saw a predator, they would *constantly* be running, leading to exhaustion and an increased risk of capture. To prevent this, zebras and wildebeests tend to flee only when they detect cues that a nearby lion is hungry or actively hunting. How, then, do these animals discern when the lion is hungry or hunting?

Prey animals gather important information by engaging in what's called predator inspection. If a predator is within range but doesn't appear to be stalking, some prey will observe the predator. Unlike

A zebra inspecting a lion. Blood on the lion's face and front leg
suggests he may not be hungry at the moment and
is likely to be less of a threat to the zebra.

humans, species without books, movies, and stories of other kinds
must rely on firsthand learning to inform them about the dangers in
their environment. Prey observe their potential predators, familiariz-
ing themselves with their appearances, habits, and behaviors. Survival
requires prey to have a certain curiosity about predators.

Predator inspection is not without its risks. As we saw in chapter 1,
animal minds perform a quick cost-benefit analysis of a situation to
guide their action when a predator is spotted. Some animals underes-
timate the speed and prowess of the predator or overestimate their own
safety while observing. One minor mistake, and the game is over.
However, if the prey survives, the knowledge it gains about predators
can be invaluable, aiding the prey throughout its life.

Zoologist Clare FitzGibbon spent two years driving around the
Serengeti, observing interactions between cheetahs and gazelles to

investigate how gazelles learn about their natural predators. She found that gazelles of all ages, except for fawns, engaged in predator inspection. However, subadults and adolescents did so most frequently. Similar to financial investing, the earlier you can (safely) begin, the better the payoff will be over your lifetime. It's no coincidence that morbid curiosity and horror fandom in humans follow a similar age trajectory, with teenagers and young adults exhibiting the highest levels of morbid curiosity on average.

Aside from age, FitzGibbon discovered other variables that made a gazelle more likely to engage in predator inspection. Gazelles that were farther away from a cheetah, part of a larger group, or near low vegetation were more likely to spend time inspecting. For humans, too, these cost-reduction factors make quite a bit of sense: Greater distance, more allies, and fewer ambush areas decrease the odds that you'll end up in the jaws of a predator.

This cost-benefit logic doesn't only apply to inspecting or learning about predators. It extends to virtually any type of threat, from dangerous individuals to treacherous locations. The less we know about a potential threat, the more beneficial it is to learn about it. Being in a safer position lowers the risk and facilitates learning. The mind efficiently identifies safe opportunities to learn about people, animals, or places that evoke danger. Our curiosity spikes to capitalize on such situations and to motivate information-gathering behavior.

The brain places an attention premium on threats because threats are important from an evolutionary perspective. To survive, we must know at least a little bit about the dangers that lurk in the dark. However, some situations are more conducive to threat learning than others. When we are relatively safe, our fear decreases and our curiosity spikes, motivating us to explore the threat. As we learn more about the threat over time, our curiosity is not piqued with quite the same intensity. The benefits of continued learning in the face of even minimal threats have diminishing returns over time.

THE WOMAN WITH NO FEAR

The amygdala, a small, almond-shaped part of the brain that is often referred to as the brain's center of defense, plays a key role in our morbid curiosity. When you perceive a possible threat, this perceptual information is routed to both the amygdala and the cortical cognitive circuits in the brain. The amygdala initiates a quick and dirty defensive response that promotes a racing heart, sweaty palms, and spikes of cortisol and heightened adrenaline levels. The cortical cognitive circuits produce the subjective feeling of fear, which is a combination of the conscious awareness of the physiological changes that are occurring (my heart is racing) and cues that something is actually dangerous (that tiger is *outside* of its cage). The defensive neural circuit that involves the amygdala is evolutionarily *very* old and can be found in various forms across the brains of all vertebrates. Defending against threats is an ancient and universal challenge for organisms, and the genes that help facilitate this have been evolving for hundreds of millions of years.

These defensive behaviors produced by the amygdala are the counterbalance to curiosity. They drive us away from danger when the costs are perceived to be too high. So what would happen if you completely removed the part of the brain that produces those defensive behaviors? Would you be left with pure information gathering in the face of a threat? Thanks to one of the most famous neurological patients in history, we have some insight into this intriguing question.

Due to a rare genetic disorder called Urbach–Wiethe disease, a patient known by the pseudonym "SM" experienced bilateral amygdala lesions as a child; her amygdala was destroyed, but the rest of her brain was left undamaged. This makes SM the perfect natural case study for how humans react to typically fearful situations without a functioning amygdala. Fortunately for science, she has agreed to participate in dozens of studies over the years. Scientists have discovered that SM is virtually unable to appropriately assess threats, and fear is absent from her emotional repertoire.

While investigating her personal history, scientists found that SM lives in a dangerous neighborhood and has been the victim of several violent incidents. In one incident, SM was walking home late at night. As she passed by a park, a man sitting on a bench beckoned her over. She walked over to the man, who immediately grabbed her by the shirt and held her down against the seat of the park bench with a knife pointed at her throat. He then leaned down and told her he was going to cut her. SM didn't panic. Rather, she calmly spoke to the man before he let her go. The next day, she took the same path home.

To better understand how she processes fearful situations, neuropsychologist Justin Feinstein and his colleagues took SM to an exotic pet store. As soon as she walked through the door, SM was drawn to the terrariums of snakes. She exhibited a childlike curiosity as she held one, rubbing its scaly skin, touching its tongue, and watching with amazement as it slithered through her hands. SM told the researchers that she was aware of the potential danger of snakes but felt no fear while handling them. When asked why she would want to hold a creature that she knew was dangerous, SM said that she was "overcome with curiosity." Without the typical defensive behaviors and feelings of fear associated with encountering a threat, she was left with only a natural curiosity for danger.

The researchers also took SM to a haunted attraction at Waverly Hills Sanatorium, which housed patients with long-term illnesses until its closure in the 1960s. Because of its historical association with illness and death, the building is a hot spot for paranormal investigators. Each year around Halloween, the sanatorium is also turned into a haunted attraction for a few weekends. For Feinstein and his colleagues, it served as a field site for a study on fear.

When they arrived at Waverly Hills, SM and the researchers were grouped with a few strangers and ushered into the haunt. SM excitedly led the group through the haunted attraction, showing no signs of fear or hesitation. When the scare actors would jump out at the group, SM would laugh while the others in her group screamed. She not only showed a lack of fear but also displayed high levels of exploratory behavior throughout the experience. The researchers noted that she actually scared one of the actors when she touched his masked face out of curiosity. Not once during the experience did SM report fear. Instead, she reported high levels of excitement that she compared to the thrill she felt when riding a roller coaster.

SM's mind shows us how curiosity is always present at some level when we are faced with a threat. In people with a properly functioning amygdala, the perceived benefits of learning about the threat must outweigh the perceived costs in order for curiosity to overcome defensive behaviors. For SM, who is unable to appropriately gauge risk, curiosity always wins out. This dynamic explains why our morbid curiosity flourishes when threats are placed in a safe context, such as in a story or playful setting.

THE (MENTALLY) TIME-TRAVELING APE

Humans are experts at mental time travel. Even if we haven't personally experienced a particular scenario, we can imagine it and project possible outcomes based on a set of criteria. If I do X, then Y might happen. The ability to ponder a simple if-then statement like this is remarkably adaptive and has incredible consequences for human behavior and evolution. It also serves as high-octane fuel for our morbid curiosity.

If I live with a small group of people in a location where wolves are prevalent, then it would be in my best interest to learn about wolves. I should try to learn where they might be found, what times of day they are most active, how to spot them, and how to evade them. One way to do this is to go out looking for wolves or to wait until I stumble across one. Of course, this is not the smartest or safest method. The risks of learning about wolves by meeting one would outweigh the benefits.

When imagination enters the picture, the possibilities for threat learning grow almost exponentially. Now I can take the information that I've learned about someone else's encounter with a wolf and apply it to a new situation. With a mental model of a wolf and how it behaves, I can imagine how it might react in various situations. By watching how my dog chases animals through the woods, I can better imagine how the wolf might hunt me if I were trekking through the forest. Known facts about wolves can be orchestrated into an entirely novel situation with a wolf that nobody has *ever* experienced. In other words, we can create and consume fictional stories about wolves that convey accurate information about the characteristics and behaviors of wolves.

Gifted with the power of language and transmissible culture, humans can share the fruits of their imagination and experience with others. As we know, threatening stories spread like wildfire compared to positive or neutral ones. Moreover, we tend to be more trusting of threat-related information. If I claimed to see a mysterious creature in the woods eating someone, that story would spread more quickly than a story about a mysterious creature in the woods eating berries. The carnivorous creature is simply more interesting due to its threatening nature. People also ascribe more knowledge and competence to others when they share threat-related information. This means that telling the story of the carnivorous creature might increase my prestige and make me seem like an important asset to the community's safety.

Humans want to hear threatening stories, and when we hear them, we want to share them. From oral stories to theatrical performances, we have numerous methods to communicate that which threatens us, and to pass this knowledge down. In many ways, our minds have been shaped by natural and cultural evolution to consume and create stories of danger. We are nature's most morbidly curious creatures.

3.

MALEFICENT MINDS

Very few of us are what we seem.

—*Agatha Christie*

AN ICY COLD CASE

In the fall of 1991, a pair of German tourists named Helmut and Erika were hiking in the beautiful Ötztal Alps on the border of Austria and Italy. Helmut and Erika were hiking at an elevation of over ten thousand feet, an altitude at which you don't expect to see much other than the serene layout of snowy mountains. Strangely enough, the couple came across what they assumed was another traveler atop the Alps. As they got closer, they realized it was a dead body, mummified in the snow. The perished mountaineer had been dead for over five thousand years.

The tourists had stumbled upon the corpse of a man who is now affectionately referred to as Ötzi the Iceman. Because he was so remarkably well mummified, we've learned quite a lot about Ötzi in the past thirty years. Carbon dating reveals that Ötzi lived during the

Copper Age, around 3200 BCE. Archaeological investigations tell us he was about five foot three, 110 pounds, and in his midforties when he died. Thanks to DNA testing, we know that his ancestors migrated to Europe from what is now Turkey around seven thousand years ago. He had brown eyes, an olive-colored complexion, and type O blood.

Ötzi didn't have the easiest life. His teeth were riddled with cavities and his insides were full of intestinal parasites at the time of his death. He also had Lyme disease and had broken his ribs and nose at some point in his life. Joints from his shoulders to his knees showed signs of crippling arthritis. Soot from long periods of sitting around a hearth covered his lungs. Despite never having eaten fast food, poor Ötzi even had hardened arteries and heart disease.

A large collection of belongings was found near his body, shedding more light on the Iceman's lifestyle. He had a cloak, leggings, two coats made from goat and sheep hide, a hat made from bear fur, and deerskin leather shoes stuffed with grass. Ötzi carried a wooden-frame backpack, a deerskin quiver full of arrows, a flint dagger, a partly finished bow, charcoal, and an unusually ornate copper ax. He was also well fed; his last meal was a mix of wheat, red deer, and ibex. The Iceman was a survivalist in every sense of the word.

For quite some time after his discovery, researchers were unsure of how or why Ötzi died. It's possible that Ötzi slipped and fell to his untimely demise. He wouldn't be the first mountaineer to suffer this fate, and his brain did show signs of hemorrhaging that appeared to stem from blunt force trauma. However, Ötzi didn't have broken arms or legs that would be indicative of a fall. The bruising on his brain also didn't appear to be serious enough to have killed him.

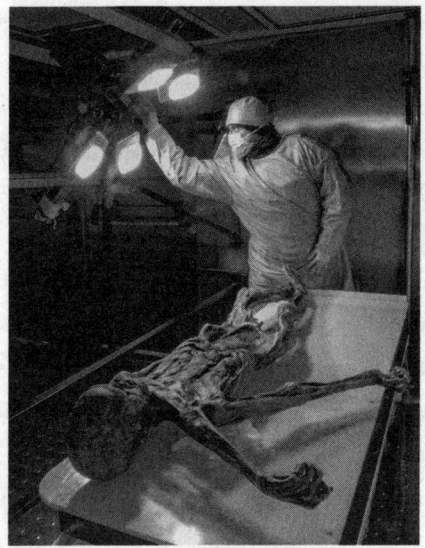

Ötzi the Iceman.

One possibility is that the brain hemorrhaging was the result of a physical conflict. Other evidence supports this theory; when he died, Ötzi's hand was still healing from what appeared to be a defensive wound caused by a dagger. However, this cut was too minor to have been a fatal wound. Ötzi's cause of death remained a mystery for nearly a decade after he was discovered. Then, a new X-ray analysis finally revealed the fatal injury: a small arrowhead lodged in his shoulder, just under his collarbone.

Ötzi had been murdered.

Newer discoveries about Ötzi's final days are painting a gruesome picture. Ötzi had the blood of four different people on his weapons and clothes. Although the current consensus is that Ötzi was brutally murdered, it's clear that he fought back, defending himself from his aggressors. It's also possible that *he* was the aggressor. Maybe he was a murderer who was chased out of town by a group of men bent on justice. In either case, one thing is certain: Ötzi is involved in one of the oldest cold case murders in history.

Our morbid curiosity about the minds of murderers motivates us to learn about and identify the signs that someone is potentially dangerous. We interrogate an individual's background, family history, and behavioral patterns to paint a picture of their potential for danger. Our ancestors who did this were better able to evade would-be murderers, passing on their morbidly curious tendencies to their offspring. Your love of true crime today is due to the success of your ancestors' curiosity about the killers among them.

A NEW TYPE OF AGGRESSION

It's remarkable that humans don't impulsively kill each other more often. Whether it's bumping into each other at a concert, standing shoulder to shoulder on city buses, or being trapped with three hundred strangers in an aluminum machine thirty thousand feet in the air, humans often find themselves in tight quarters with total strangers. Violent incidents do occur from time to time, but millions of encounters like this happen every day with relatively few acts of aggression. We take this for granted, but it's a peculiar phenomenon for a primate. Evolutionary anthropologist Sarah Hrdy once remarked that if a plane full of chimpanzees ever managed to leave the tarmac, it would be a miracle if any of them survived the flight unmaimed. The aisles would be flowing with blood and severed body parts by the time the plane landed.

To be clear, humans can be aggressive. But we are not aggressive in the same way that chimpanzees or other primates are aggressive. Chimpanzees, like many primates, have a social hierarchy that is enforced through reactive aggression. If a chimpanzee challenges or doesn't defer to a chimpanzee of higher rank, the higher-ranked individual will respond violently. The bigger, stronger chimpanzee is reactively aggressive because this quick, violent response to a transgression works well to maintain power in chimpanzee hierarchies. Human hierarchies don't usually work like this. Social rules often regulate reactive aggression and punish those who can't control their violent outbursts. Moreover, humans are by their very nature less reactively aggressive than other primates.

Biological anthropologist Richard Wrangham argues that humans have low levels of reactive aggression because they have domesticated themselves. What's more, Wrangham contends that humans did this by killing off overly aggressive males. Now, I know how this sounds. It seems paradoxical to say that humans used violence to become less aggressive over time (hence the title of Wrangham's book *The Goodness Paradox*). Killing aggressive males requires aggression, so how could this have led to the domestication of our species?

The answer lies in the fact that there are two main kinds of aggression. I've already mentioned reactive aggression, the impulsive response to a perceived threat that is fueled by anger and fear. This is the default type of aggression across the animal kingdom, and many animals have high levels of reactive aggression. The other type of aggression is called proactive aggression. Rather than being impulsive in nature, it's colder and more calculating. It requires planning and foresight, skills at which humans excel.

Most human societies make clear demarcations between these

two forms of aggression. In the US justice system, proactive aggression that leads to the death of the victim is considered first-degree murder. A criminal convicted of first-degree murder can be subject to the harshest possible punishments: either life imprisonment without parole or death. Those who kill out of reactive aggression, where no planning was involved, cannot be sentenced to death in the United States. They will still be punished and will likely spend years or even decades in prison. However, the punishment for someone who kills reactively is not as harsh as the punishment for premeditated murder.

The distinction between the two types of aggression goes deeper than the justice system; it is rooted in our biology. Although social and contextual factors influence reactive and proactive aggression, these two types of aggression are mediated by somewhat distinct areas of the brain.

Neurobiologist Adrian Raine has conducted pioneering neuroimaging work on convicted murderers to better understand the biological roots of violence. In one study, Raine scanned the brains of murderers who had committed either reactive homicide or proactive homicide. An example of reactive homicide would be coming home to find your wife in bed with another man and killing your wife's lover in a fit of anger. The murder in this case is driven by impulsive rage. An example of proactive homicide would be finding out that your wife is cheating on you and then planning for days or weeks before killing her lover.

Prisoners in Raine's study who committed murder out of reactive aggression showed lower activity in their prefrontal cortex than prisoners who committed premeditated homicide. Unsurprisingly, this part of the brain plays a major role in inhibition and impulsivity. Compared to control subjects who were not murderers, both re-active and proactive murderers displayed greater activity in the limbic regions of the brain. These regions of the brain mediate emo-tional responses, such as anger and rage. So, convicted murderers had greater activity in areas of the brain that mediate rage, and those who killed out of reactive aggression had less activity in the area of the brain that inhibits impulsivity. It's important to mention that just because you have "more activity" in the limbic regions of the brain or "less activity" in the prefrontal region, it doesn't mean you'll be a murderer. One way to think about this is that these neurologi-cal features help produce the right conditions for murder. Other fac-tors, both biological and environmental, help shape whether or not someone becomes a killer.

Because proactive aggression and reactive aggression are medi-ated by different neural substrates, it is possible for one type of ag-gression or the other to become more common in a population throughout evolutionary time. In our species' deep past, reactively aggressive males were the norm, just as they were in many other pri-mate species. However, beginning around three hundred thousand years ago, natural selection produced a solution for our hotheaded ancestors who acted as tyrants over their groups. With the emer-gence of language, cooperation became more feasible, and groups of males could conspire in secret to overthrow more reactively aggres-sive males who were in power. One consequence of this shift was that those aggressive despots had fewer offspring, and the children who inherited their reactively aggressive tendencies would face the same fate as their fathers. Traits that promoted reactive aggression were now "bad" from an evolutionary standpoint because they led to decreased reproduction and survival. Over thousands of generations, the genetic predispositions for reactive aggression slowly faded from the gene pool. This is the basis of Wrangham's *Goodness Paradox*: We became less reactively violent by cooperatively planning to violently overthrow reactively aggressive males.

The males who were cooperating to overthrow the reactively aggressive males were also increasing their own reproductive fitness. Not every male in a group would have participated in the coups. Those who participated would have needed some tendency toward aggression while simultaneously possessing some impulse control. This led to a selection pressure for more individuals with a propensity for traits like impulse control and cooperation—and more people with a predisposition for cold, calculated murder.

NEW SIGNS OF DANGER

Like many other primates, our ancestors were able to identify dangerous males through signals that had evolved to communicate reactive aggression. Some of these signals were behavioral: possessing a short temper, lashing out in response to fear or anger, and behaving dominantly in social situations. When we see these behaviors in an individual, we know to be wary of their aggressive tendencies. The shift from reactive to proactive aggression in our species rendered many signals of aggression less useful. It also created a new problem: There were now many more proactively aggressive people lurking about. Instead of a propensity for aggression being exposed in social situations, it was now hidden away in the mind, festering until the time was right to strike. Quiet, premeditated killers now prowled among us.

The capacity for premeditated aggression can even be seen in those of us who are not killers. Psychologist David Buss and his colleagues demonstrated this in a massive international study that included over five thousand individuals from a variety of different cultures. The researchers asked these thousands of people if they had ever fantasized about killing someone and, if so, to describe the fantasy. They came across a shocking discovery: 91 percent of men and 84 percent of women recalled having at least one vivid fantasy in their lifetime about murdering someone. Despite the fact that the global murder rate is exceptionally low, the psychological mechanisms that can produce proactive aggression and can lead to homicide are churning away in the minds of nearly every person. If the circumstances were right, who knows how many of these fantasies would materialize.

A NATURAL HISTORY OF TRUE CRIME

The urge to understand the mind of a murderer can be almost irresistible. This desire—this morbid curiosity—fuels the popularity of the modern-day genre of true crime. However, the thirst to understand dangerous people is not a modern phenomenon. Early versions of stories that we recognize today as true crime were sung in medieval ballads and transmitted through oral stories around the nightly fire. It wasn't long after the invention of the printing press that written stories resembling modern-day true crime began to emerge. Sensational and graphic stories of murder filled the pages of pamphlets beginning in the 1500s. One of the early examples of this came from author and Lutheran minister Burkard Waldis. In 1551, Waldis published a story of how a woman savagely murdered her four children:

> *She first went for the eldest son*
> *Attempting to cut off his head;*
> *He quickly to the window sped*
> *To try if he could creep outside;*
> *By the legs she pulled him back inside*
> *And threw him down on the ground;*
> *He got up and away he did bound.*

The story continues with the mother chasing her eldest son, ax in hand. She eventually finds him hiding in the cellar and hacks away at him. Her other three children suffer equally gruesome fates before she kills herself and the terror comes to an end.

The story carefully describes the scenes and the children's attempts to escape. Readers devoured the details of this gruesome story, despite already knowing the outcome from the overly descriptive title: "A true and most horrifying account of how a woman tyrannically murdered her four children and also killed herself, at Weidenhausen near Eschwege in Hesse." With access to vivid details of how the woman murdered her children and how the children failed to escape, readers could imagine for themselves what they might have done differently. Would they have escaped the house alive, or would their deranged mother have hacked them to bits in the cellar?

Dangerous situations are compelling on their own, but the psychological motivations of the killer are a key ingredient of true crime's success. People want to know what the killer was thinking, how they acted before the crime was committed, and if they gave any clues about their violent nature. This more psychologically centered version of the true crime story rose to prominence in English ballads and pamphlets in the late sixteenth century. The focus of the story shifted from the description of the crime itself to the mind of the person who committed the crime. Advances in psychology over the past century have led to an even greater emphasis on descriptions of the killer's motives. Because we have the scientific ability to better understand the minds of killers today, the public hungers for this information.

The structure of modern living has also contributed to the rise of true crime and the allure of the dangerous man next door. For nearly all of human history, people knew their neighbors quite well. Neighbors were family members, friends, and other members of a tighter-knit group. You would hunt, gather, feast, and engage in communal rituals with your neighbors on a regular basis. Strangers certainly existed, and you interacted with them, but they did not live next door, and they certainly did not make up the majority of those surrounding you like they do in a modern city. Strangers were also not treated the same as members of your local community. With their intentions unknown, strangers would be met with skepticism and caution.

As populations grew, people in many parts of the world began living in closer proximity to strangers than any of their ancestors could have imagined. Today, many of us are surrounded by people we don't know at all. We still deal with this much better than our primate cousins would, often giving strangers the benefit of the doubt when it comes to following the norms of society. Crammed trains and fully booked restaurants exist without descending into chaos. However, the potential of a dangerous stranger still lurks in the back of our mind. Most of us don't assume our neighbor is a killer, but sometimes his behavior might have us wondering if he has bodies in his basement.

The fear of the murderous everyman living in our neighborhood was crystallized in the minds of many Americans in the latter half of the twentieth century. It was a time before sophisticated forensic techniques had been developed, and criminals didn't need to worry about leaving DNA behind at crime scenes. For a handful of psychopathic killers, this meant hunting season.

In the 1970s, several young women began disappearing or were found murdered in Washington, Utah, and Colorado. These women had strong social networks around them and were not the type to simply vanish without informing their friends and family. The bodies that were found had been brutally beaten and ravaged. The crime scenes were gruesome. No average man could have committed these atrocities.

By all appearances, Theodore "Ted" Bundy was an average man. He was a charming and handsome law student who had worked as a political campaign activist. Bundy was often described as smart and mild mannered, and spent time volunteering at a suicide help hotline. He gave no indications that he was anything other than an ordinary guy. Despite his everyman appearance, Bundy murdered dozens of young women across the western United States over the span of only a few years. His crimes were clearly premeditated and often involved deception. One of his ruses involved disarming women by pretending that he had an injury. Other times he would impersonate someone, such as a police officer, to gain the trust of his victims.

Around the same time that women were disappearing across Washington, Utah, and Colorado, several young men and boys in the Chicago area were also being reported as missing.

John Wayne Gacy moved to the Chicago area in the 1970s and quickly became a respected member of the community. He founded a successful construction company but still found time to visit kids at hospitals and birthday parties dressed as a clown whom he called Pogo. He frequently threw neighborhood summer parties at his home and was active in local politics, serving as a Democratic precinct captain. Through his involvement in his neighborhood, Gacy became a well-known and well-liked member of his community. He also brutally tortured and killed over two dozen young men and boys, burying most of them in a crawl space under his house. Like Bundy, Gacy used premeditation and deception to lure his victims to their untimely deaths. He would encourage his victims to visit his house under the pretense of discussing work and place them in compromising positions under the guise of demonstrating a magic trick.

Stories of these well-respected and seemingly normal men committing horrendous murders flooded the news. Two malicious serial killers had camouflaged themselves as trusted members of their communities, all while they stalked and killed dozens of innocent people. Strangers became a feared threat, and our curiosity about potential murderers among us skyrocketed. By the end of the twentieth century, the potential danger of strangers became solidified in the minds of many Americans. Wide faces, large brow ridges, and tense interpersonal interactions weren't helpful for predicting this manner of killer. To identify and avoid predatory men like Bundy and Gacy, you need a better understanding of their minds and behaviors. You need morbid curiosity.

The morbid curiosity that emerged out of this new reality has fueled the rise in popularity of true crime media that explores the lives and minds of serial killers at length. The killer's loved ones are interviewed, often remarking that they can't believe their friend or family member would do such a thing. Their childhood is scrutinized, with investigators digging deep to find any threads that link their experiences as a child to their murderous behavior as an adult. Psychiatrists and forensic psychologists are often interviewed to get a grasp on what the inner life of such a monster is like. These insights into the killer's mind tug at the morbidly curious strings of our own minds and are key to the success of the true crime genre.

A DOUBLE-EDGED BLADE

Some conspiracies do exist. One of the earliest recorded and most famous examples of a conspiracy was the murder of Julius Caesar. Caesar's decision to declare himself dictator of Rome wasn't very popular among many of his political contemporaries. Out of fear that he was capturing too much power, a group of over twenty senators hatched a plot to murder him. At the Senate meeting on March 15, 44 BCE, Caesar was ambushed by the conspirators and stabbed over twenty times, changing the course of Roman, and perhaps all of European, history.

Caesar wasn't alone in falling victim to a conspiracy. Many famous conspiracies either changed the course of history or would have if they hadn't been foiled. Who knows how history would have played out if Guy Fawkes and his conspirators had succeeded in their assassination attempt on King James I. Or how the twentieth century might have unfolded if the July 20 plot to assassinate Adolf Hitler had succeeded. Numerous assassination attempts have been made on American presidents, a few successful and several unsuccessful. Although many conspiracies that people are familiar with involve political leaders, conspiracies can happen to anyone—strangers conspiring to rob you, rivals conspiring to kill you, or coworkers plotting your career demise.

In its most basic form, a conspiracy involves a person or group of people plotting to harm another person. The key word here is "plotting": A conspiracy is an act of premeditated aggression. Once language evolved, groups of people could work together to conspire against a rival. These conspiracies to commit violence against another person were at the heart of the reduction in reactive aggression among early human ancestors. It was targeted, conspiratorial murder that group members engaged in against the reactively aggressive males. Our curiosity about the minds of dangerous people shares its origins with our interest in conspiracy theories.

Morbid curiosity can act as a preventative measure against premeditated or conspiratorial aggression. Empowered with the urge to learn more about potentially dangerous people, we are able to keep the edge against dangerous people and potential conspiracies that might be brewing against us. However, this same proclivity for seeking out information about the minds of potential conspirators can sometimes put us at risk of buying into conspiracy theories that have little grounding in reality. It's the smoke detector principle all over again; better to see a few conspiracies where there aren't any than to miss a true conspiracy. Taken too far, this can spin us into paranoia and lead to wildly unfounded beliefs.

We don't know why Ötzi the Iceman was killed. He could have been a criminal stealing from a small village or a murdering psychopath fleeing from the town he had been massacring. A bit of morbid curiosity may have led a group of individuals to become suspicious of Ötzi and catch on to his killer nature. Or maybe Ötzi was a good man. He might have been a local leader who wielded power and resources that others desired so strongly that they plotted to murder him. If so, perhaps a little more curiosity about the minds and motivations of dangerous men would have served Ötzi well in his final days.

4.

PARANORMAL PERCEPTIONS

The oldest and strongest emotion of mankind is fear,
and the oldest and strongest kind of fear is
fear of the unknown.

—H. P. Lovecraft

FINDING WHAT ISN'T THERE

Savannah, Georgia, is widely considered one of the most haunted cities in the United States. The city's spooky reputation stems from a long history of death, disease, and destruction dating back to its founding in 1733. Savannah was a major slave trade port in the 1700s and the site of one of the bloodiest battles of the American Revolutionary War. It was hit with numerous yellow fever outbreaks in the 1800s, with the first outbreak claiming an eerie 666 lives. The yellow fever outbreaks were so deadly that multiple mass graves had to be dug for the victims. If war, slavery, and disease weren't enough, one of the deadliest hurricanes in US history nearly destroyed the city in the late 1800s. As a consequence of its gruesome history, there are many more corpses buried under Savannah than there should be for any city of its size. It's a city built on bodies, and many people believe that the spirits of those poor souls have stuck around.

So, of course, I had to visit.

It was on a cool November night that I found myself taking part in a paranormal investigation at the Old Sorrel–Weed House in Savannah. The Sorrel–Weed House is a beautiful sixteen-thousand-square-foot mansion built in 1840. The house was built upon the location of the bloody Revolutionary War battle, the Siege of Savannah; hundreds of bodies still lie buried beneath its basement. The original owner of the house, Francis Sorrel, was a rich and powerful citizen of Savannah in the mid-nineteenth century. At some point in his marriage, his wife, Matilda, discovered that Francis was having a sexual relationship with an enslaved woman named Molly. Distraught, Matilda ran to the balcony of the mansion and leapt to her death. Because she was a slave, Molly knew she would be held responsible for the socialite's death. Days after Matilda's death, Molly was found hanged in the carriage house in an apparent suicide. Complete with infidelity, suicide, and a mass grave, it's no wonder that the Sorrel–Weed House is well known for its paranormal activity and is regularly ranked as one of the most haunted places in the United States.

At around 11:00 p.m., our group of six investigators began wandering through several of the rooms in the house. We carried with us various instruments that are supposed to aid in the detection of ghosts and spirits. Many of the instruments measured aspects of the environment that paranormal beings might be able to interact with. For example, we had digital air thermometers so that we could see if an area of the room suddenly got cold: a classic sign that a spirit is nearby.

Small seismographic instruments allowed us to measure vibrations or movements on the floor. Each investigator was also given a simple handheld radio. According to some paranormal investigators, quickly skipping through the channels on a radio is one way to detect verbal responses from spirits. One of the more intriguing devices we had was called a REM pod. The REM pod is a small box with an antenna that emits a local electromagnetic field. If something—for example, a ghost—interferes with that electromagnetic field, the REM pod buzzes and lights up on the side that was disturbed.

We witnessed an occasional disruption in the REM pod's magnetic field and odd temperature fluctuations throughout the night. At one point, the seismograph detected movement when we asked a ghost to knock in affirmation of a question. However, as interactive as they were, our fancy gadgets were no match for our natural sensory instruments. Nothing makes you feel the presence of a ghost like your own sense of sight, sound, and touch. And nowhere was this as clear as it was in the dark and unnerving basement of the Sorrel–Weed House.

I got chills twice during the night, and I was in the basement both times this happened. The basement of the Sorrel–Weed House is reportedly one of the most paranormally active areas of the estate. Despite not being a believer myself, I still find paranormal investigations to be quite fun. In many ways, paranormal investigations are a bit like imaginative play for me; a way to engage my morbid curiosity. Still, in the throes of a midnight ghost hunt in one of the most haunted places in the world, my senses were on high alert for potential danger.

At one point during our basement investigation, I was standing near a lonely side table. It was fairly dark, but I could tell that no-body in our group was within a few feet of me. Suddenly, I felt a very clear brush on my right leg, as if someone had run their fingers across it. I quickly turned around and looked behind me to see . . . nothing. Goose bumps immediately filled my body. I, or at least some part of my mind, *knew* that nothing had touched me. But a different part of my mind had other ideas about what had happened. Just seconds later, another one of the investigators let out a small yelp. She had felt something touch her hand not far from where I was standing.

People often report detecting the ghosts of small children in the basement of the Sorrel–Weed House. Visitors commonly say they felt as if someone tugged on their pant leg or brushed up against their hand as they searched through the dimly lit basement. Although it gives them a startle, people aren't usually too afraid when they feel a brush on their hand or tug of their pants in the basement. After all, they're ghost children. How dangerous could they be?

However, the children aren't the only ghosts in the basement. A much more menacing spirit is said to reside in the shadows of the basement. The apparition that people see is often described as resembling a tall middle-aged man in a period-appropriate uniform. He is believed by many to be the spirit of a long-dead Revolutionary War soldier who was buried under the foundation of the home after the Siege of Savannah.

A long, uninterrupted stretch of floor encased by a wall with two doorways runs along one edge of the basement. At one end is a single wooden chair, positioned such that it is looking down a dark cavity of the hallway. Apparently, the soldier is often spotted in this area of the basement. One man from our group decided to sit in the chair and see if he could see or hear anything. After only a minute or so, he walked through the doorway closest to the chair looking visibly shaken. He didn't say much other than he was sure he saw a shadowy figure staring back at him in the hallway.

Intrigued by this, I decided to go sit in the chair for myself. After all, ghosts don't exist.

Right?

My mind was telling me that ghosts don't exist, but my body was reacting as if this soldier was very real, very angry, and waiting for

The basement hallway
in the Sorrel–Weed House.

me in the hallway. I sat alone in the chair, staring down the long, dark hallway. My eyes darted back and forth—did I see a shadow? Was that a face? My mind raced through possible scenarios. I got an uneasy feeling that was difficult to explain and even harder to shake. It felt as if something was wrong, but I couldn't identify what it was. I don't think I saw the ghost of the soldier because I don't believe that ghosts exist. But some part of my mind was convinced that something might be out there in the dark, and it was telling my eyes to be vigilant. Each time I thought I saw something, my mind latched on to the idea that it was most likely the soldier's ghost. My heart raced at each shifty shadow. I kept telling myself it was nothing, but the threat detector in my mind simply wasn't having it.

Why were my mind and body reacting as if the ghost of the soldier was in the room even though I don't believe in ghosts? Why couldn't I help but see and feel what I knew wasn't there?

A HAUNTING IN THE MIND

Psychologist Jesse Bering and his colleagues have shown that I'm not alone in this dissonant experience. The researchers conducted a set of studies to see if belief in the afterlife affected how someone responded to the potential presence of a ghost. The logic was simple: If someone doesn't believe in an afterlife, then they shouldn't react to the potential presence of a ghost. After all, if there is nothing after death, that should exclude the possibility of ghosts sticking around.

In their first study, the researchers recruited participants for what was ostensibly a meditation study. At least one day before they came to the lab, the participants completed a questionnaire at home that assessed the extent of their belief in an afterlife. When the participants arrived at the lab, half of them were told that a university janitor had recently died in the testing room they were in. The participants were assured that there was no risk to their safety, but informed that they must sign a "notice of death on premises" form. After they signed the form, the researcher leading the study casually mentioned that a PhD student swore they recently saw a ghost in the testing room. The other half of the participants, who were in the control condition, were not told anything about a death or ghost in the room.

When you're in a fearful situation, your body becomes more physiologically aroused. As part of this process to prepare you for fight or flight, your heart rate increases and you begin to sweat slightly, the latter of which increases the electrical conductance of your skin. Because of this, your heart rate and skin conductance can be used as proxy measures of how physiologically aroused, and how prepared for fight or flight, you are. The researchers took advantage of this and hooked up the participants to instruments that measured both heart rate and skin conductance. They then left the participants alone in the room, where they listened to a nine-minute recording on how to engage in mindfulness. The physiological instruments were allegedly measuring how relaxed the participants were; in reality, the instruments were measuring how afraid they were of ghosts.

After the mindfulness recording finished, the participants were asked to sit in complete silence for six minutes and use the mindfulness tools they had just learned to contemplate a problem they were experiencing in life. During this task, each participant sat alone in a quiet room that was illuminated only by a small desk lamp. In the middle of the six-minute meditation task, a researcher in another room surreptitiously turned off the lamp using a remote control. The participant sat in complete darkness for seven seconds before the light turned back on.

As it turns out, a flickering light is a bit scarier when someone tells you a ghost was recently seen in the room. Participants in the experimental group, who were told about the death of the janitor and the reports of a ghost in the room, had higher heart rate and greater skin conductance after the light-flickering incident than did those in the control group who didn't hear anything about a death or ghost in the room. Participants who heard about the ghost were subconsciously preparing for danger, and their physiology was showing it.

Interestingly, a participant's physiological response to the flickering light didn't depend on their belief in an afterlife. Afterlife believers and nonbelievers alike showed increased physiological arousal in response to the light flickering in the experimental condition. While the nonbelievers may not have consciously believed that a ghost caused the light to flicker, their minds and bodies responded as if an otherworldly agent was responsible for the disturbance. Much like my creepy experience with the soldier's ghost in the basement, the nonbelievers in this study couldn't help but feel uneasy. The parts of their mind that manage threat monitoring were on high alert.

A SPOOKED SPECIES

National survey data suggests that most people believe in at least one aspect of the paranormal. According to a Gallup survey, over half of Americans believe in psychic or spiritual healing, two out of every five believe in extrasensory perception, and around a third believe that houses can be haunted and that ghosts or spirits of the deceased can come back in certain places and situations. Although it has a strong pop-cultural presence these days, astrology trailed behind several other paranormal beliefs, with 25 percent believing that the position of the stars and planets can affect people's lives.

Altogether, nearly three out of every four Americans hold some type of paranormal belief. And as we've seen, even the minority of people who report not believing in the paranormal in any way may act differently when a potentially paranormal situation arises. It's easy to walk around in the light of day and say ghosts don't exist; it's much harder in an old basement with a reputation for paranormal disturbances. It is in these creepy places that conscious effort and belief can sometimes be at odds with cognitive biases that have been etched into the blueprint of our brains over millions of years of evolution.

Americans aren't alone here. All human cultures have some concept of the paranormal, whether it's ghosts, deities, or ancestral spirits. If we take the skeptical view that ghosts, spirits, and other paranormal entities don't exist, then the prevalence of paranormal beliefs across cultures and throughout time is an interesting puzzle. Why would humans have this seemingly useless ability—tendency, even—to perceive and believe in things that aren't readily seen? How could this aptitude have been beneficial enough to become a universally evolved feature of the human mind?

One influential theory about why we perceive and believe in the paranormal comes from psychologist Justin Barrett. He has argued that humans hyperactively detect agency. This means that humans are likely to ascribe events in the world, such as a rustling sound in the leaves or a strange shadow on the wall, to living entities with intentions behind their actions. In other words, we have a tendency to see purpose behind events, even when those events are sometimes merely coincidences. The reasoning is the same smoke detector principle that we've seen before: It's generally better to be safe than sorry. Assuming that some event is caused by an agent with intentions and goals isn't very costly. It's better in the long run to err on the side of that quiet rustling in the bush being caused by a stealthy predator than to assume it is just the wind.

What we experience is shaped by our expectations. I don't believe in ghosts, so my baseline expectation is that I will not see one. However, I was taking part in a paranormal investigation when I was exploring the Sorrel–Weed House, and everyone else there was actively searching for paranormal entities. Despite my conscious disbelief, the context in which I found myself set my mind up to perceive any potential evidence of a ghost. If I had been walking through the house as part of a historical tour, and especially if I had done so in the daytime and without knowing the house was famously haunted, my experience would have been quite different. The expectation that the estate was haunted, and investigating it in the dark, biased my mind toward detecting something lurking in the shadows.

My colleagues at the Recreational Fear Lab have shown how expectations and environmental context can influence our sensitivity to agency detection. Marc Andersen and his team had participants travel through a forest in virtual reality and asked them to press a button each time they saw a being. Half of the participants were told they had a 95 percent chance of encountering a being in the forest while the other half were told they had only a 5 percent chance. Each participant virtually walked through one part of the forest where the weather was clear (high visibility) and a section where the weather was misty and foggy (low visibility). This means there were four total conditions:

1. High chance of an encounter in high visibility
2. High chance of an encounter in low visibility
3. Low chance of an encounter in high visibility
4. Low chance of an encounter in low visibility

Participants who were told that there was a 5 percent chance they would encounter a being were much less likely to press the button to indicate that they saw one during the study. Even in the low-visibility portion of the forest, most participants did not report seeing anything. However, in the condition where participants were told there was a 95 percent chance they would see a being, *most* participants clicked the button at some point during the walk. When the participants were in the misty and foggy part of the forest, they were even more likely to report having seen something, and many participants in this condition indicated that they saw multiple beings during their virtual walk.

So how many beings were actually in the forest in each condition?

Zero. There was nothing in the forest in any of the conditions.

However, prior expectations and sensory uncertainty made some participants more likely to believe they saw something. Their minds avoided false negatives (missing something in the forest when it was there) at the expense of generating more false positives (seeing something that wasn't actually there). If I had been in the Sorrel–Weed basement during the day and without knowledge that it was haunted, I may not have even noticed those slight changes in lighting and temperature. The faint feeling that something brushed my hand would have been treated as a random sensation or an unseen cobweb rather than the ghost of a playful child.

Our tendency to hyperactively detect agency plays an important role in our tendency to experience and believe in the paranormal, and this tendency feeds our morbid curiosity. However, as we just saw, hyperactive agency detection is dependent upon our preexisting conceptions. We need to have a concept of the paranormal in order to detect it. If paranormal entities didn't exist in one's culture or mental model of the world, then being on high alert for an agent would lead to something like paranoia rather than a paranormal experience. In other words, hyperactive agency detection amplifies our preexisting paranormal beliefs and experiences, but we need other cognitive mechanisms to fully explain our belief in, fear of, and eventual curiosity about paranormal beings.

PARANORMAL WITH A PURPOSE

Other people are often the cause of phenomena that affect our lives. Because of this, we have evolved the ability to predict others' intentions and actions. We need to have a sense of why people act the way that they do so that we can find allies, identify enemies, and resolve conflicts. If someone intentionally spills their coffee on me, that's a lot different than if someone accidentally knocks their coffee cup over and some of it spills on me. It comes naturally to us, so we don't usually notice it, but our day-to-day social life depends on our ability to identify intentions behind other people's actions. This is known as theory of mind.

By attributing to other people the mental faculties that inspire action, including thoughts, intentions, beliefs, emotions, and desires, we can better predict their behaviors and engage in complex social interactions. Importantly, theory of mind involves the ability to understand that others can have *different* thoughts, intentions, beliefs, emotions, and desires than you do. This is key to human sociality and cooperation, and natural selection has carved out neural circuits in the human brain to be highly specialized in theory of mind. Interestingly, these same brain regions are active when we reason about the intentions and emotions of nonhuman beings. If you try to understand why your cat knocked the remote off the side table for the hundredth time, you use many of the same neural circuits that you'd use if your spouse knocked the remote off the side table. What or who we reason about doesn't matter much for these brain regions. Their function is to parse information that can give clues about an agent's intention and emotions.

Our closest primate relatives don't appear to have this mind-reading superpower in the same way that we do. Developmental psychologist Masako Myowa-Yamakoshi demonstrated this in a study with both human and chimpanzee participants. She used a specialized instrument to track the eye movements of humans and chimps while they viewed a video of a woman performing a goal-directed action. In the video, the woman is seated at a table with a bottle of water and a cup. The woman picks up the bottle and pours the liquid out next to the cup, spilling it on the table. When chimpanzees watched this video, their eyes focused on the bottle and the cup; they focused on the affordances of the objects (bottles and cups hold water) and the end goal of the action (pouring water). The chimpanzees didn't spend much time looking at the woman who was engaging in this action.

Human eyes told a different story. When humans watched this video, they looked at the bottle and the cup, as the chimpanzees did. However, they also looked at the woman's face as she poured the water onto the table. The human participants were looking for intention in the woman's face—things like gaze direction and facial expressions of surprise or satisfaction. These nonverbal cues can be used to infer if she is intentionally or accidentally pouring the water out on the table. While a look of surprise may indicate an accident, a smirk may indicate mischievous intent. Humans and chimpanzees both gather information about objects involved in a goal-directed action, but humans take it a step further and integrate object information with social information.

Our inclination to look for intention in actions is so strong that we often see intention where it doesn't exist. We apply this perception bias so broadly that we don't need to be looking at humanlike beings in order to perceive intention. We don't even need *living* beings for this bias to occur. This tendency to overperceive intention in action is demonstrated by a classic study where participants watch a video of two dots moving on a screen. The dots move all around the screen, with one dot following directly in the path of the other.

When people are asked to describe what they see, most of them report that the trailing dot is chasing the leading one and trying to catch it. Dots on a screen obviously don't possess agency. However, people can't help but attribute purpose to their movement. The visual input of one thing moving directly behind another is a format that our mind has evolved to interpret as a chase.

Assumptions about intentions, beliefs, and desires give us an anchor for making sense of other people's behaviors. They're jumping-off points for the inferential systems in our mind. Without these assumptions, *anything* could be a possible explanation for other people's behavior. If we want to know why a man murdered another man, we need to have some intuitive assumptions about why he did it in order to constrain the world of possible explanations. If we didn't, then any one explanation would seem as likely as another; "he did it because he had pasta for dinner" would be just as likely to pop into our minds as "he did it because he was angry." We would need to evaluate a nearly impossible number of potential causes if we didn't have an intuitive anchor of some kind.

The assumption that people behave according to their desires and beliefs is a simple anchor that radically constrains the list of possible reasons for another person's behavior. This gives us a starting point for understanding other minds and often leads to true-enough beliefs that allow us to behave in ways that are adaptive. When we combine this premise with contextual information that we gather (e.g., the guy he murdered insulted him first) and our ability to imagine how we would feel or react in a similar situation, we get an efficient model that is surprisingly good at understanding and predicting other agents.

One consequence of this intuition is that we sometimes believe that events that aren't easily ascribed to another human are caused by a paranormal or supernatural agent. Because threat-related information has such a powerful grip on our minds, misfortunate events in particular prod us to find a responsible agent, with the blame often falling on powerful paranormal entities. However, we don't ascribe paranormal or supernatural explanations to all misfortunate events equally. A team of psychologists led by Joshua Jackson and Danica Dillion dug deep into the ethnographic record to see if cultures were more likely to ascribe supernatural explanations to unfortunate social phenomena (such as murder, warfare, theft) or unfortunate natural phenomena (such as lightning, fire, disease). The study was impressively comprehensive and included ethnographic reports from over one hundred cultures across the world.

The researchers found that people were much more likely to ascribe supernatural causation to natural phenomena than social phenomena. This was true across different types of cultures, including hunter-gatherers, horticulturalists, pastoralists, and agriculturalists. Many social misfortunes, such as war, theft, and murder, can be readily explained by human agents; there is usually no need to invoke the paranormal to explain how terrible people can be. Interestingly, the researchers found one exception to this trend: In socially complex societies where people didn't know their neighbors as well, there was a higher tendency to attribute supernatural explanations to some social events. It's much more difficult to explain people's behavior when you don't know much about them.

Misfortunate natural events such as floods and wildfires aren't readily or easily explained by human actions. A dangerous or angry man is not the obvious choice to blame for a flood or a drought. After all, a typical angry person doesn't control the weather. Still, our minds are biased to interpret these events as the consequences of an agent with intentions and desires—such as an angry deity with the power to control the weather.

THE SOCIAL FORMAT

Our tendency to believe that mysterious agents with intentions and desires are the cause of dangerous or unfortunate events leads us to be morbidly curious about the paranormal. Even when a natural cause is available, our mind begs for an agential explanation. Many times, people are willing to accept both natural and paranormal explanations of the same event; paranormal explanations of events are not always, or even usually, mutually exclusive with natural explanations. You can understand natural proximate causes for phenomena and still believe that paranormal intervention was the ultimate cause. One of my favorite examples of this was told by anthropologist Alma Gottlieb.

During her time living among the Beng people in West Africa, Gottlieb knew that she should boil her water to rid it of parasites and other harmful microorganisms. This was especially important in the village she was staying in because it was experiencing a terrible Guinea-worm outbreak from polluted drinking water. Gottlieb tried to convince her neighbors to boil their water to protect themselves from the outbreak, but they simply laughed it off.

The Beng believed that the outbreak of illness was caused by malevolent witches. When Gottlieb insisted that the cause was worms, her Beng friend simply asked, "Can you see the worms in our water?" Of course, Gottlieb could not see the worms since the parasites are transmitted to humans as larvae inside of small water fleas. Her friend finally conceded that maybe there were small, nearly invisible worms in the water. However, he maintained that boiling the water would do no good because "boiling the water won't stop the witches."

When it comes to explanations of events, people are often more interested in why the event occurred rather than how it occurred. *Why* did this happen to me instead of *how* did this happen to me. "Why" questions are alluring because if we assume an individual is behind some event, knowing the "why" gives us information about their intentions and how to deal with them. If I know why someone honked at me on the highway, I can decide if it was a legitimate reason or not. If I know why a flood occurred in my area, I may be able to take steps to prevent future floods from occurring. Searching for the answer to why something happened uses the human superpower of causal reasoning. But it can be misapplied when we incorrectly assume an agent is responsible for an event.

The human mind has been designed by natural selection to better understand and navigate social interactions because social interactions are the most important and frequent type of interaction we experience. As a result, we often use the format of a social interaction as the default way to think and reason about things. One example of this default state of reasoning is assuming that an event is caused by another living being rather than a consequence of environmental or otherwise natural causes. This means the explanations we search for involve possible reasons an individual would do something ("the generous crop yield this year was due to our piety pleasing God"). If a misfortunate event occurs, the format of the explanation our mind searches for is a social violation ("God caused this flood to occur because he was angry that we didn't sacrifice a goat"). We assume gods, spirits, aliens, and other paranormal forces possess and act on their beliefs, intentions, and desires, just as we do with other humans. God caused the flood because he was angry with us, not because he had pasta for dinner.

To understand this more clearly, let's look at an example of a built-in format bias in our technology. If you've ever used Microsoft Excel, you've probably found yourself frustrated at least once at the way it interprets almost any number combination and certain word combinations as dates. Excel does this because its default setting is to interpret numbers and certain word combinations using the format of date entries.

This assumed formatting in Excel has caused problems in the field of genetics. Many genes have long, descriptive names that would be inconvenient to read and write. Because of this, most genes have commonly used abbreviations. For example, "membrane-associated ring finger (C3HC4) 1, E3 ubiquitin protein ligase" is a real mouthful. Rather than using its formal name, molecular biologists and geneticists have shortened it to the much simpler "MARCH1" moniker.

As you might have guessed, Excel assumes MARCH1 is a date by default and interprets it as March 1. Apparently, it's not uncommon for gene acronyms like MARCH1 and SEPT2 (Septin 2) to be misinterpreted as dates by Excel. One study found that nearly 20 percent(!) of published genomics papers had at least one gene name that Excel had inadvertently interpreted as a date. Since statistical analyses work only on number-formatted cells, data in those misinterpreted cells wouldn't be included in the analysis or final interpretation of the results.

Despite the troubles it causes, the date-conversion bias presumably helps more than it hurts, or else Microsoft would have removed this feature. Although geneticists don't use dates too often in their spreadsheets, dates are a very common and important aspect of spreadsheets for Excel-heavy jobs like bookkeeping—common and important enough that it makes sense for the default interpretation of certain entries to be dates.

The human mind's inferential system works much like Excel, only our bias is to interpret certain inputs as the result of actions by another person. When we try to understand why something happened, we tend to interpret the cause through the lens, or format, of social interaction. Much like Excel forces date formats on many text and number entries, we often impose a social format onto actions. This bias allows complex social interactions to flourish with ease. But it also enables paranormal beliefs to arise.

THE PERFECT PARANORMAL STORM

Living things that conceal themselves are implicitly assumed to be nefarious—think of a cougar hiding stealthily beneath the tall grass or a man peeking around a corner. Neither of these is initially assumed to be friendly and well-intentioned. Instead, we suspect they are intentionally cloaking themselves from our view because they are trying to harm us. We often assume the same of paranormal beings, which by their very nature are difficult to detect. Ghosts and aliens aren't usually perceived as neutral or friendly agential beings. Rather, they are often initially seen as evil or threatening. Casper is a rare exception of friendliness in the paranormal world.

We can't easily learn about ghosts, spirits, or aliens because they are hidden from our view. Whether they're in an astral plane, on another planet, or living in a grand hall in the sky, their ability to exist outside of our perception leads us to assume they are powerful and likely dangerous. We want to know more about the ghost who sneaks around the old house or the alien who visits in the dead of night. We see them as potential threats that we need to learn about, just like the stealthy cougar or the shifty man in the dark alley. This fuels our morbid curiosity for them.

5.

VICARIOUS VIOLENCE

I feel myself ashamed and degraded at the brutal
curiosity which took me to that brutal sight.

—*William Makepeace Thackeray*

A BREWING CONTROVERSY

In the early 1990s, video games were captivating players of all ages
and emerging as a mainstream form of interactive entertainment.
Previously popular in arcades, video games began to be made for
platforms that could be purchased and played inside the home. As
the industry blossomed, so too did concerns about the impact of violent video games on society, particularly on the impressionable
minds of young players.

One game in particular emerged as a lightning rod for this
mounting controversy. Released in 1992 by Midway Games, *Mortal
Kombat* broke new ground with its cutting-edge graphics, intense
combat, and unabashed display of gore. The game's fatalities—
graphic finishing moves that allowed players to execute gruesome
and visceral attacks on their opponents—became the subject of

fascination by players and outcry by others. *Mortal Kombat*'s violence was unprecedented in gaming, displaying massive amounts of blood, bone-crushing impacts, and explicit brutality.

The depictions of extreme violence were simply too much for Nintendo and the family-friendly approach to video games it had cultivated for its gaming platform. However, Nintendo didn't want to miss out on the anticipated success of *Mortal Kombat*. As a compromise, it published the game on its SNES with a few key changes. The red, pixelated blood that spouted from fighters was changed to gray and referred to in-game as sweat. Fatalities were renamed "finishing moves" and had their gruesomeness toned down considerably, with a few of them being changed entirely. Nintendo hoped this compromise would help the company maintain its family-friendly integrity while also allowing it to capitalize on an exciting new game.

Mortal Kombat was also published on the Sega Genesis system. However, Sega didn't have the same ethical dilemma with pixelated blood or with characters ripping the spines out of their enemies. When *Mortal Kombat* was released on the Sega Genesis, it was playable in all of its gruesome glory. This decision ended up being a smart move. The uncensored Sega version of *Mortal Kombat* outsold the sanitized Nintendo version *five to one* in its first month, despite the Sega Genesis being vastly outnumbered by the Nintendo SNES in American households.

As *Mortal Kombat* gained popularity among young players, the controversy surrounding the game intensified. It didn't take long for it to catch the attention of concerned parents, educators, and politicians. The media seized upon the sensationalism, with headlines decrying the corrupting influence of violent video games. The game's graphic violence and perceived lack of moral boundaries ignited a fierce debate about the potential impact of such content on the minds of young players. Parents and educators worried that these virtual realms of bloodshed were degrading the moral compass of a generation, leading children down a path of desensitization and aggression at home and in school.

The moral panic surrounding violent video games filled the pages of academic journals for years and spurred millions of dollars in grant funding. Hundreds of researchers were asking the same question: Does playing violent video games make kids more violent? This research focus extended well into the early 2000s and resulted in one of the most intensely investigated and highly contested topics in the history of psychology. The conclusion of this campaign is now clear: Violent video games do not make children more violent. Fantasy can feel real at times, but humans can easily distinguish between what is real and what is not. Excitedly smashing buttons on a controller does not make a kid more likely to be aggressive in the real world.

Although millions of dollars were spent investigating whether violent video games make kids aggressive, very little research was conducted looking at why violent video games were so appealing in the first place. Why did the uncensored version of *Mortal Kombat* sell five times as many copies as the sanitized version? What draws people to virtual realms of bloodshed and brutality in books, movies, and video games? Why do humans find themselves captivated and curious about violence? Since nobody else seemed to be working on this puzzle of human nature, I decided to tackle it in my work.

FINDING THE CORE OF MORBID CURIOSITY

When I began my PhD program, one of the topics I spent a lot of time thinking about was violence. What intrigued me about this topic was that violence is largely considered wrong. Many acts of violence violate moral codes and result in social punishment. Yet, society has carved out specific areas where violence is not only unpunished but serves as socially sanctioned entertainment.

Multibillion-dollar sports like boxing and MMA specifically center around acts of violence. However, instead of repulsing their audiences, these sports draw in spectators by the millions. And this phenomenon isn't new. The Roman Colosseum, one of the largest structures in the world when it was constructed in 80 CE, was built largely as a venue for violent entertainment. On a busy day, nearly eighty thousand Romans would pack the stands of the Colosseum to witness brutal and bloody gladiatorial fights. Although many gladiators were slaves, the most skilled and violent fighters were celebrated as heroes, and the crowds would chant their names in admiration.

What is it about violence that is also so alluring?

The threat of violence sits at the core of morbid curiosity. It's adaptive for humans to know about threats because they have the potential to enact harm upon us, and this is bad from an evolutionary standpoint. There are several different ways to learn about violence, and many of these opportunities are indirect. We may learn about the physical or behavioral cues of dangerous men, the nature of maleficent spirits, or the bodily injuries that result from a dangerous encounter. All of these give us clues about how to recognize, deal with, or avoid something dangerous. We can remove the high cost of learning about violence directly by simulating it. We can watch it on television, read about it in a story, experience it in a video game, view it from the stands of a stadium, and safely engage with it through other types of simulations.

PIERCING THE MIND'S VEIL

In evolutionary biology, behaviors can be categorized as proximate or ultimate. However, evolution has built proximate motivations that encourage us to pursue behaviors that are ultimately good for us. Our immediate experience of seeing a pus-filled infectious wound is a visceral feeling of disgust and repulsion. We don't need to think about why it is disgusting in order to avoid it. In fact, it's often difficult to articulate why. The ultimate reason for many of our behaviors is hidden behind the veil of our immediate experience.

Rough-and-tumble play is a great example of this. Many young mammals, including human children, engage in play that safely emulates violent experiences. Kittens and puppies nip and paw at each other in ways that appear quite rough but are relatively safe unless greater force is applied. Children, especially boys, wrestle with each other and simulate violent encounters in a playful way. Even seemingly innocent games such as the chase-based game tag or the hunting game of hide-and-seek are, at their core, playful ways to practice predator escape maneuvers.

In humans, coalitional or group aggression is a key threat in adulthood. Wars, skirmishes, and raiding parties have been common among human societies throughout history. Unsurprisingly, we often see simulations of coalitional fighting in children and young adults through sports like football or playground games like red rover. By playing these team-oriented games, kids and young adults can engage in simulations that employ critical features of dangerous, real-world threats.

Proximate reasons for engaging in rough-and-tumble play or violent simulations can make them seem superficial. "I play them because they are exciting" doesn't exactly hit at the importance of these activities. But these motivations evolved to help our species survive and thrive. The ultimate or evolutionary reason humans get enjoyment out of violent media and play is because they are a safe way to learn about and mentally practice dangerous experiences. Evolution has crafted our minds to be intrigued by violence so that we pay attention to it and learn about it when we are in a safe position to do so.

A deeper analysis of proximate reasons (the conscious motivations and thoughts) for engaging in a behavior can sometimes shed light on the ultimate (or evolutionarily functional) reasons a behavior exists. To better understand people's motivations for consuming media violence, Anne Bartsch and her colleagues interviewed people about their experience with violent movies. The researchers identified three main themes that led to engagement with and enjoyment of violent content: truth value, real-world relevance, and psychological and moral implications.

When participants spoke about truth value in Bartsch's studies, they tended to mention learning and confronting the dark reality of certain situations. Violent media is often brutally transparent about how a dangerous situation might look, leaving little to the imagination. Participants reported that this unvarnished depiction was an important part of the appeal.

One of the subthemes within truth value was the ability to safely explore real-world situations that are otherwise inaccessible due to how dangerous they are. War movies are a great example of this. You could learn what it's like to fight your enemies by enlisting in the military and being deployed during a war. Although you would gain unique perspective and insight into a dangerous situation by doing this, it obviously occurs at great potential cost to your own safety. Alternatively, watching a realistic war movie is a safe way to glean *some* insight into this dangerous situation. You won't have the same understanding of war as a person who actually fought in one, but you would have more insight into it than someone who has never fought in a war, never seen a war movie, and never read a book about war. Stories are no substitute for the real thing, but that doesn't mean they don't carry truth value and the potential to learn something useful.

The second major theme that emerged in Bartsch's research was real-world relevance. This refers to the fact that some of the information being consumed is not only truthful but relevant. Despite stories not capturing the full experience of being in a dangerous situation, their real-world relevance is sometimes quite obvious. One participant in the study noted,

> Let's use this SS officer as an example: You should know such extreme situations and you should be ready to intervene, so that such situations won't happen in real life.

Some of the participants were in the military at the time of the study and explicitly mentioned watching war-related media to learn more about how other military operations have occurred. Other participants mentioned imagining how they would respond in dangerous situations portrayed on-screen. Movies, like other forms of stories, offer a useful way to simulate dangerous experiences. As we'll see in chapter 9, the real-world relevance of movies like *Contagion* became clear during the COVID-19 pandemic.

The final major theme that emerged in Bartsch's study was the psychological and moral implications of violent media content. Some violent situations are morally ambiguous and prompt viewers to consider the motivations of those who engage in violent behavior. One participant discussed this, saying,

> I mean, it makes a difference whether it's a serial killer running around killing people by chance or if it's someone with certain values, someone who is blinded by values and thus kills people. If someone like the latter kills people it is, in my opinion, more understandable as compared to someone who fires indiscriminately.

This theme also connects to the "minds of dangerous people" domain of morbid curiosity from chapter 3. Stories that are psychologically real, meaning they depict realistic actions and behaviors, can offer incredible insight into the minds and behaviors of violent people.

The three reflective themes about violent media—truth value, real-world relevance, and psychological and moral implications—

align with the theoretical foundations of morbid curiosity about violence. Our ancestors who indulged in their curiosity about violence and who explored it through safe simulations were better prepared to navigate violent ordeals that they would likely one day face.

Our attraction to violence might seem paradoxical in some ways. The same action may be seen as virtuous by one person or one culture, and barbaric by another. A duel in the Wild West might have been seen as honorable by many American cowboys but brutish by our modern standards. An act of violence can even be seen as praiseworthy in a specific situation but heinous by the same culture in a different situation. A Roman piercing his blade through another is seen as commendable by the Romans when it happens in the Colosseum but treasonous when it happens at the Forum.

One of the first scientific studies I conducted showed that violence is one of the few things that is powerful enough to draw our attention away from faces in a scene. I had participants in my study view a wide range of social interactions between two or more people while I tracked where they were looking on the screen. These photos had been pre-rated as being either violent or nonviolent. For example, a nonviolent photo might show two men giving each other a high five, while a violent photo would show two men fighting. In each of these cases, there was a point of contact being made between two people: a handshake or a punch. When participants viewed scenes that were rated as more violent, they spent much more time looking at the point of contact. In other words, the violent act itself captured people's attention in a powerful way.

We don't have to be instructed to look at violence, just like we don't have to be instructed to look at faces. We do it instinctively. Looking at violence doesn't mean we necessarily like it or approve of it. But this does suggest that it is an important part of social life, and that it is something beneficial to pay attention to and be curious about.

A VIOLENT PAST

It's a common misconception that our hunter-gatherer ancestors existed in a state of peace compared to modern societies. I won't dive too deep into the evolution of human violence here, but it's worth noting a few key facts.

It's no secret that many modern cities have high rates of violence. In the US, cities like New Orleans, St. Louis, and Baltimore consistently average around 60–70 homicides per 100,000 people. This is far above the national homicide rate, which hovers around 8 homicides per 100,000. Some cities outside of the US rank even higher; Tijuana, Mexico, averages around 100 homicides per 100,000 people. But how do these numbers compare to homicide rates throughout human history?

It's difficult to get accurate estimates of violence in the past. We can look at indicators, like the percentage of skeletons we've found that have lethal wounds, but this is a noisy signal. Not all homicides leave evidence on the bones, and homicide victims might not be buried and preserved in the same way as those who died from other causes. We can also look at written records of homicides in major cities or countries, but some places have kept better records than others over the years. Still, we have enough converging evidence to create reasonably well-informed estimates.

Cognitive psychologist Steven Pinker has famously (or infamously, depending on your camp) argued that violence has declined steadily over the course of human history. Pinker outlines hundreds of pages of empirical evidence for his claim in his massive tome *The Better Angels of Our Nature.* Looking at countries in Europe that have reliable estimates, Pinker presents evidence from numerous scholars showing that countries like England, Italy, Germany, and the Netherlands had *countrywide* homicide rates around 1200 CE that matched modern-day Tijuana. However, homicide rates have declined in those countries from around 100 per 100,000 in 1200 CE to around 1 per 100,000 in the twenty-first century.

For modern nonstate societies like the Waorani of Ecuador or the Yanomami of Brazil, scholars often rely on accounts of homicide or skirmishes reported by missionaries or anthropologists who live among the groups. Estimated rates of homicide among modern nonstate societies range from around 30 per 100,000 to around 100 per 100,000; they're as lethally violent as some of the most dangerous cities in the world. The caveat here is that these societies are much smaller in size than a typical city, so a few homicides per year can result in a high rate of death by violence. Still, over 10 percent of deaths in these societies result from violent conflicts (compared to just 1 percent for the US and Europe).

All animals engage in violence to some degree, and humans are no exception. In fact, we are pretty much as violent as science predicts a social ape would be. José María Gómez and his colleagues demonstrated this when they conducted a phylogenetic analysis of lethal violence among mammals. The researchers gathered and analyzed sources of mortality among mammals to identify what percentage of each mammal species dies at the hands (or paws, or teeth, or horns) of a member of the same species. They created a phylogenetic model, or algorithm, that could predict the rate of lethal violence in humans based on the animal data they had collected.

The model estimated that the percentage of human deaths attributed to lethal violence would be around 2 percent. The team then looked at empirical evidence of rates of lethal violence from the archaeological record to see how well their phylogenetic model performed. Just as their model predicted, empirical evidence of human lethal violence over the past fifty thousand years was estimated to be around 2 percent of all deaths.

Two percent of all deaths is nothing to shrug at. It may seem small compared to something like cancer, which is closer to 9 percent, or heart disease, which is closer to 17 percent. However, cancer and heart disease typically take the lives of older adults, whereas homicide occurs more often in younger adults of reproductive age. It's also worth keeping in mind that we have much more control over our chances of dying of homicide than of cancer or heart disease. The causes of cancer and heart disease are multifaceted and occur over long periods of time, making them difficult to predict and prevent. However, the factors that precipitate homicide are often clear enough that we can take steps to avoid it, and natural selection can more easily act upon these factors. One of the behavioral traits that can help counter the threat of lethal violence is to be curious about it, learn why it transpires, and identify tactics for avoiding it.

VIOLENCE IN THE SOCIAL WORLD

Humans are highly social creatures who rely on one another for survival. We evolved from primates who were social by nature, and they evolved from primates who were social by nature. Millions of years of living among other members of our species have etched certain psychological and behavioral tendencies into our DNA, including a curiosity about violence that occurs in the context of social life.

When an individual breaks the social mold by taking the life of another person, we feel compelled to ask what led to it. In some cases, the violence is instrumental; the killer wanted something, and murder was the way to get it. Psychopaths are a good example of the type of person who might engage in instrumental violence. However, psychopathic killers are somewhat rare, and lethal violence is often not instrumental in this way. In many instances, a violent act occurs because the perpetrator feels as if it's the right thing to do. They feel they *must* engage in violence to create, sustain, modulate, or terminate the social relationship.

This idea isn't as far-fetched as it sounds. Violence is an integral part of social relationships in animals. Most animals use violence as one way to negotiate relationships. When an alpha chimp wants something that a beta chimp has, the alpha chimp doesn't negotiate with words; he negotiates with muscular forearms and menacing canine teeth. In fact, *that is why those anatomical features exist.* Large canine teeth evolved because of their ability to enact violence or the threat of violence. That's not to say all chimpanzees are violent to the same degree. They have a variety of temperaments just like humans do, with some being more prone to aggression than others.

But violence is the medium through which many social decisions in chimps and other social animals are made.

Violence is an important aspect of human relationships. Anthropologist Alan Fiske and moral psychologist Tage Rai make this argument in their book, *Virtuous Violence*. This book was eye-opening for me as a graduate student trying to understand why humans are sometimes violent and why that violence could spark our curiosity. The central argument of the book—that violence is seen as necessary and even moral by many perpetrators—is not as controversial as it seems. For many people across the world and throughout history, violence is an acceptable way to regulate social relationships, especially those where a transgression has occurred.

Dominance or authority hierarchies are one example of a social relationship where violence is sometimes seen as acceptable. Authorities often use violence to regulate social relationships. You see this when the alpha chimp bites a lower-ranking chimp for getting too greedy with food, a parent disciplines a child for disobeying the rules, or the state executes a criminal for a murderous act. Still, being in a position of authority does not give unilateral rights to violence. Legitimate authority figures can and sometimes do abuse their power to enact violence.

This potential for abuse is one reason why violence is important to pay attention to and be curious about. Humans live in complex societies, and it's easy for bad deeds to get swept under the rug when nobody is looking. We need to keep tabs on authority figures to ensure they are not using their power to enact violence in a way that is threatening to us or our group. We need to be curious about violence to keep abreast of amoral or illegitimate violence.

Violence or the threat of violence was also an important feature in the evolution of group living. Group living provides increased safety from predators and access to potential mates, but it comes at the cost of fighting over resources.

Because fighting is costly, even for the winner, many group-living animals use dominance hierarchies to determine resource allocation. Your rank in the hierarchy is typically determined by how formidable you are in an aggressive conflict, which can be indexed fairly accurately by how large you are. If you come upon a piece of fruit at the same time as someone ranked lower than you, then you get the fruit; if they are ranked higher than you, then they get the fruit.

Dominance hierarchies are a clever trick of nature, but they don't completely solve the problem of intragroup violence. The ranking of the hierarchy isn't static; sometimes it's unclear which organism is more formidable and brief conflicts erupt to determine the ranking. Many times, these conflicts will take the form of ritualized aggression, which involves two animals flaunting their formidability, like two men puffing up their chests and yelling at each other, or two gorillas pounding their fists against their chests. This gives competitors the opportunity to (literally) size up the competition. Signals of size, strength, and aggression give an idea of who might win if a conflict occurs. If the two animals do not come to an agreement about who would win based on the posturing, then flaunting may escalate into a violent conflict to determine who is higher in status and gets the resource. For witnesses, this information is critical.

Herein lies another reason why violence is alluring: Violent conflict gives insight into how well our estimation of one's formidability maps onto their actual formidability. This is particularly important since the ritualized aggression that acts as the glue of the hierarchy offers only an *estimate* of formidability. A violent conflict, on the other hand, puts the puffed-up chests and flexing to the test. It's a bit like a poker player who bets big for a few hands, leading the rest of the table to fold. Eventually, you want someone to play through the end of a round just to see the player's hand. If you do this enough times, you'll become better at predicting when someone is bluffing. Similarly, if you witness enough violence, you'll be less naïve when it comes to predicting how dangerous someone or something really is.

Violence is dangerous and scary, and this is why it's so interesting to us. It's a central means by which animals negotiate resources, whether that's food, territory, or mates. Humans may have found alternative ways to navigate status and resource allocation, but violence has still been central to power shifts, both big and small, throughout our species' history.

We are inclined to observe acts of violence because they convey important information about the true formidability and skill of potentially dangerous individuals. This exposure makes us less naïve about how violent someone might be. Being curious about violence also better equips us to deal with a potentially violent situation if one were to occur.

Our ancestors had to exercise caution when observing violent acts, lest they become a victim of the violence they were witnessing. In the modern world, acts of violence are simulated through stories, television shows, movies, and video games. This simulated violence can be consumed at virtually no risk, making it a magnet for our morbidly curious minds.

6.

INTRIGUING INJURIES

Leontius felt an overwhelming desire to
look at the bodies while simultaneously
loathing the thought of them.

—Plato

A GRUESOME SPECTACLE

The *Indiana Jones* movies were my favorite movies when I was a kid. I still love them as an adult, and I've lost count of how many times I've seen them. I never could remember which titles went with which stories when I was young, so I referred to them by their content. For example, the one where the bad guy pulls out the man's heart (*The Temple of Doom*). Or the one where the bad guys' heads melt and explode (*Raiders of the Lost Ark*).

Those bloody scenes weren't the only reason I watched, but they were the most memorable parts of the movies. Anyone who has seen *Raiders of the Lost Ark* remembers when the Nazi's face melts like an ice cream cone on a hot summer day. Those scenes were shocking and had me asking all sorts of questions about the human body and the dangerous things that cause injury to it. Can a face really melt like that? Could a religious relic really kill you? Is it possible for someone actually pull your heart right out of your chest? The bodily injuries that were depicted in the movies were gory, and I would sometimes experience a feeling of disgust when I saw them. At the same time, they filled me with fascination. Those gruesome scenes were stirring my morbid curiosity.

When I talk with people about horror movies, one of the most common lines I hear is, "I find horror interesting, but I just can't do gore!" It's a fair concern. Since a horror story usually revolves around a monster or killer of some sort, it's likely the audience will witness some blood and bodily injuries. After all, bloody injuries are what monsters and killers do best. But how gory are horror movies, really? If you were to estimate how many minutes of on-screen gore occurred in a typical ninety-minute horror movie, what would be your guess?

The answer is probably less than you think. Media scholars Blair Davis and Kial Natale conducted an ambitious ~~horror movie marathon~~ research study where they documented every second of gore in one hundred horror movies released in theaters between 1998 and 2007. While this study didn't account for the prime slasher era in the 1980s, it did capture the "torture porn" era of the early 2000s, the face of which included gruesome movies like *Hostel*, *Saw*, and *House of 1000 Corpses*.

The average time of on-screen gore in the sample was a measly four minutes. This number included *all* instances of gore, including passive scenes that depicted only blood. Active gore, where a character was actively being injured, averaged only around fifty seconds per film. In other words, the average horror movie had a couple of violent scenes involving the killer and a handful of scenes where the bloody aftermath was shown. I'm not sure how this compares to other genres, but I suspect there are plenty of action movies and crime dramas with more than fifty seconds of violence and four minutes of bloody fallout.

Although there are a few outliers with extra buckets of blood and severed limbs, the average horror film simply isn't that gory. In fact, some horror films terrify viewers with basically no gore—*The Conjuring*, *The Blair Witch Project*, and *Insidious* come to mind. Still, many scary stories have at least a few bloody scenes that draw furrowed brows and curled upper lips from the audience. Despite experiencing disgust and sometimes fear, people keep coming back for more. That's because bodily injuries also elicit fascination, excitement, and intrigue.

VISCERAL FEAR

Master of horror Stephen King argues that there are three kinds of scares that can be used to frighten the audience: the *Terror*, the *Horror*, and the *Gross-Out*. Each of these types of scares serves a different purpose and incites a different reaction from the audience.

The *Terror* lives in our mind. It's the feeling of unease we get during the tense buildup in a psychological thriller. The *Terror* is related to the fear of the unknown, which H. P. Lovecraft famously deemed the oldest and strongest fear of mankind. Our imagination fills the gaps of the unknown with our greatest fears, and a good horror writer takes advantage of this, shepherding the audience's minds to their own worst fears without actually showing the monster.

If the *Terror* lives in the mind, the *Horror* lives in the eyes. The

Horror happens when the monster bursts onto the scene. The *Terror* is the slow buildup, and the *Horror* is the jump scare. It's the manifestation of the dread that the audience has been experiencing. The *Horror* relies on evolved signals of danger to scare the audience; the sharp claws, big teeth, bladed weapons, physicality, and predatory nature of monsters tap into evolutionarily old parts of the brain that evolved to help us detect danger. Michael Myers stalking his victim is reminiscent of a lion's prowl. Dracula's fangs resemble the canine teeth that hang from the mouths of creatures that have preyed upon humans throughout time. These features are reliable cues of a horrifying creature.

The final level is the *Gross-Out*. The *Gross-Out* lives in the gut. It's the outcome of the monster's violence: the torn limbs, the buckets of blood, and the scattered entrails that make your stomach turn. The visual aspect of the *Gross-Out* produces immediate disgust, the only level to do so. But the *Gross-Out* can also produce fear. Seeing bloodied guts strewn across the floor begs for an answer to the question, "What kind of terrible monster could have done *this*?" If the monster hasn't yet appeared in the story, imagining the terrible beast that caused the *Gross-Out* can lead to anxiety-dripping *Terror*, fueling the cycle of fear.

King calls the *Terror* the highest form of fear that the horror writer can achieve. I'm not one to argue with the master of horror about his craft. King might be right here. However, the *Gross-Out* can serve as high-octane fuel for the *Terror*. Severed limbs and pools of blood set the scene for imagining the most dreadful of monsters. Death and grievous bodily injuries are why we fear monsters, killers, and other kinds of dangerous predators in the first place.

We evolved to be curious about dangers that cause bodily injuries because they have a powerful impact on our survival and reproduction. One of the best ways to avoid threats like this is by detecting them before they detect you. The *Gross-Out*—those bodily injuries, blood, and other remnants of an attack—signals to us that a dangerous being is out there. It's adaptive to attend to those stomach-turning signals, and feeling intrigued or curious motivates us to learn more about them.

The *Gross-Out* gives us a gauge of how dangerous the threat really is. It serves as a visceral reminder that what we are facing is a force to be reckoned with. The more destroyed the body is, the more terrifyingly powerful the monster is imagined to be. If I come across a corpse with a slit throat, I don't get a clear signal of how big or powerful the monster is. But if I come across a corpse with a smashed head, I'm really going to be afraid. An injury like that requires serious aggression and strength. Our estimation of a threat's power and danger is directly related to the amount of damage it can do to the body. This is a key reason why bodily injuries demand our attention and arouse our morbid curiosity.

The signaling power of the *Gross-Out* is especially effective for threats that aren't overtly dangerous. Samara, the black-haired spirit from *The Ring*, doesn't express any physical indications of extreme power. Sure, she's creepy, but she's small in stature and doesn't carry a weapon. However, she signals her true power through the film's notorious *Gross-Out*. Samara's victims are left with their jaws snapped open and stretched diagonally beyond the limits of what seems possible. It's a *Gross-Out* that reflects the danger that Samara poses, and one that still haunts those who have seen the film.

The *Gross-Out* also affects our attitude toward certain infectious diseases. Diseases that cause noticeable bodily damage provoke more fear than those that are inconspicuous killers. Ebola is an especially terrifying disease in part because the symptoms of infection can be horrifying. Although many who perish from Ebola die of dehydration, severe cases can really demonstrate the destructive power of the disease. When someone succumbs to an extreme case, their body looks as if they had been attacked by a monstrous beast; profuse bleeding from the eyes and mouth is reminiscent of an attack by a powerful predator. These visual cues engage parts of the fear system that other diseases fail to trigger, creating a more visceral horror.

WHY SO GRUESOME?

History books are bursting at the seams with violence. Wars. Brutal rituals. Homicides. Humans are violent creatures. However, we aren't just violent; we are sometimes *gruesomely* violent. Some of the most hauntingly memorable scenes of violence in human history are excessive in nature. This is the kind of violence that goes beyond just defeating your enemy, like Vlad the Impaler earning his epithet by mounting his enemies on spikes.

Several years ago, I became interested in why humans are sometimes gruesomely violent. There were plenty of explanations for typical human violence available: It's an effective way to bend others to your will, prevent someone from taking precious resources, or defend yourself in times of danger. However, there were no satisfying explanations for why someone might be gruesomely violent. Why gut someone and pull their intestines outside of their body? Why behead them and put their heads on a spike? It takes extra energy to be gruesomely violent, and it takes effort to overcome the disgust and empathic response that naturally results from this type of violence. So, why do people sometimes do it?

One reason a killer might be gruesomely violent is that the killer wants to signal something to others. By doing excessive damage to the body, the killer is making a statement. They're telling potential future enemies that they mean business. Governments and ruling classes are notorious for this. Extremely gruesome public executions, such as drawing and quartering, send a clear message to would-be deviants. The mangled nature of the corpses gives us the feeling that whoever or whatever was responsible is incredibly powerful.

Body size reliably predicts success in conflicts across the animal kingdom; larger opponents are likely to be more dangerous. This is why lions are more frightening than house cats and why wolves are more frightening than Chihuahuas. This is also why horror villains such as Jason Voorhees, Michael Myers, and Leatherface are all big guys. Their size influences how formidable they appear. If Leatherface was five feet tall, the chase scenes in *The Texas Chain Saw Massacre* just wouldn't hit the same.

Although size is the biggest predictor of conflict success, other factors can also influence the outcome. In humans, our ability to win fights is a combination of physical factors (including size and muscularity), social factors (like allies and martial arts training), technological factors (such as weapons and armor), and psychological factors (like motivation or aggression). All else equal, a person with many allies will defeat a lone enemy. A well-armed individual will overcome an unarmed opponent. An aggressive, motivated man will outcompete a meeker rival.

Despite all these factors influencing the outcome of an aggressive encounter, the mind still uses physical size as its blueprint to estimate fighting success. Evolutionary anthropologist Dan Fessler has conducted numerous studies showing that we inflate a person's size in our mind's eye if that person possesses other factors that influence success in conflict. For example, a man holding a gun is perceived to be physically larger than a man holding a less lethal object. Our mind utilizes the format that evolved for assessing strength (i.e., body size) to process and make decisions about conflict-related information.

This got me thinking: Could gruesome violence also make us envision a perpetrator as larger and stronger? If so, this might explain why some aggressors enact gruesome violence on their enemies. I teamed up with Dan Fessler to find out.

We recruited participants for our study and had them read stories about two men who came into conflict with each other. In some variants of the stories, the winner of the conflict gruesomely defiled the enemy's corpse after killing him. We then had the participants estimate some of the winner's physical and psychological traits. People who read the stories where the winning man was gruesomely violent estimated him to be larger, stronger, and more aggressive than people who read the violent but non-gruesome stories. People also believed that the gruesome antagonist would be more likely to win future fights. This held true across multiple stories with different kinds of perpetrators. Gruesomeness was conveying information about the formidability of the perpetrator.

Much like violent encounters, tales of ghosts, and the minds of killers, bodily injuries offer important insight into threats we may encounter. Consequently, we are morbidly curious about them.

PROOF OF DEATH

Deep cultural knowledge and sophisticated tools help modern humans identify the living from the dead. At the most advanced level, we might determine if someone is dead by using an electroencephalography, or EEG, to check for brain activity. There's a deeper philosophical question about what death really means here, but it's safe to say that, in general, a lack of brain activity in an organism indicates death. At a less technological level, we might check for a pulse by placing our fingers against someone's neck. No pulse, no life. Knowing if a person is dead or alive isn't a huge problem in today's world, but it hasn't always been this way.

Animals don't have EEGs. They don't know how to check for a pulse. For much of our history, humans faced this same problem. Before the invention of the stethoscope in the 1800s, humans would check breathing by holding a feather under the nose or placing a mirror near the mouth to check for condensation from breath. However, this method can fail in sickly individuals with shallow breathing. Our early ancestors likely wouldn't have known to check for breath as a sign of life. In fact, debates raged in the medical community as late as the 1700s about whether or not putrefaction might be the only sure sign of death. In other words, our ancestors faced a major problem: How do we know if another person or animal is dead?

Let's imagine a wolf died outside your home. If you didn't have a way to identify the wolf as dead, you might spend a lot of time trapped inside. You would go on living as if the wolf were alive, remaining on high alert and afraid to go outside. Assuming the wolf was alive would waste time that could be spent gathering precious resources or engaging in other fitness-enhancing activities. If you recall from chapter 2, this would be like a zebra assuming every lion they see is hungry and on the hunt.

In another example, let's imagine a child in the household has died. For most of human history, children had staggeringly high mortality rates, and I do mean staggeringly high. By some estimates, approximately *half* of all children died before puberty in historical societies. Children are more susceptible to certain diseases and to predators than adults, so childhood deaths were exceptionally common. Without a good way to identify when a child has died, we might continue behaving as if a dead child were alive. We would continue gathering resources for the deceased child and waste time trying to care for it at the expense of ourselves and our other children. Problems like this are common enough that the mind needs a way to identify when someone is likely to be deceased.

The cognitive switch between believing a person or animal is living and believing it is dead is difficult to flip. Anthropologist Clark Barrett and psychologist Tanya Behne have argued that the switch is "sticky" because it's usually more costly to erroneously assume something is dead when it's actually alive. If we assume a child is dead when she goes to sleep, we'd stop caring for her. If we assume a lion is dead when it's actually asleep, we put ourselves at risk of attack. Because of this, the switch from believing something is living to believing it is dead should require strong cues and be difficult to enact. Immobility, for example, is a weak cue of death. Dead things are always immobile, but living things are sometimes immobile as well.

One strong cue that can flip the mind's switch to categorize something from living to dead is a grievous injury. Psychologist Claire White and her colleagues tested the idea that serious bodily injuries are a clear cue of death in a study using recently deceased pets. For humans, a pet dog or cat can occupy a special place as a family member or companion. We often treat a pet like we would treat a fellow human (sometimes even better!). Because of this strong emotional attachment, losing a dog or cat can sometimes feel like losing a family member. We grieve, bury, and memorialize pets like we do other humans.

White and her colleagues recruited participants at veterinarian offices in the US and UK who had recently lost a dog or cat. The researchers asked participants about their attachment to their pet, how long ago the pet passed away, and the nature of their pet's death. Did they see the pet's body after it died? Was the body intact (e.g., if it died by euthanasia), or was it physically injured (e.g., if it died in a car accident). Finally, the participants explained in their own words how they knew that their pet was dead.

The researchers were testing the idea that false recognition (mistaking sights and sounds as coming from a recently deceased loved one) might be lower if the corpse had severe bodily injuries. False recognition is a fairly common occurrence after a death. If you lived with a partner for several years before their passing, you could be forgiven for initially mistaking a sound in the kitchen as coming from them preparing a meal.

White's team found that attachment to the pet and how recent its death was were both related to the frequency of false recognitions. However, seeing a non-intact corpse was the strongest predictor of experiencing fewer false recognitions. Those who saw the physically injured body of their pet were much less likely to misperceive sights and sounds as coming from their recently deceased pet.

The comparison here might be between a dog struck by a vehicle and a dog who was put to sleep in old age. When an animal is put to sleep, it simply looks like it is sleeping; the visual cues of death are weak. However, when a pet is hit by a car, the visual cues of death are clear. According to White and her colleagues, bodily injuries on the corpse help us understand that an animal is dead.

Though it is more traumatic and sorrowful in the moment, seeing a grievous injury might actually help us move through the grief process more efficiently. This has interesting implications for the funeral industry. In the United States, death, or any indication of it, is often pushed as far away as possible. We don't want to see the body of a deceased loved one until their makeup is done—until they look almost alive again. Funeral professionals spend countless hours ensuring that everything about a deceased person looks . . . not deceased. Their hair and makeup are perfected to ensure a lively appearance. They are dressed in their finest clothes and jewelry, as if they were about to go out for dinner. And any visible sign of injury is covered up with wax to emulate unscathed skin. And, if all these measures fail due to a grievous injury that prevents a lifelike reconstruction of the corpse, we simply keep the funeral casket closed. These measures might help make us feel better in the moment, but they could also be slowing our progression through the grieving process.

Different cultures often have wildly different ideas about how to deal with the dead. The deceased might be buried in one culture, embalmed and kept in the home in another, and burned in a pyre in another. Funerals are sometimes celebrations of life, with dancing, food, and music. Other times, they are ceremonies of mourning with tears and solemn remembrances. Funerals can be brief, or the funeral games may last for days. The rites within a culture can also vary by class, gender, or occupation. The diversity of human cultural experience is manifest through funerary rites.

Despite these differences, there are some universal attributes of funeral rituals. The dead are typically treated with respect through a ritualized norm, whether that comes from solemn remembrance or fires and dancing. The body of the deceased usually undergoes some sort of preparation for the funeral. This may include dressing the corpse, applying makeup, preserving the body, "feeding" the corpse, and a number of other actions that require close contact with the body. In the United States, these preparatory funerary rites are outsourced to a professional class; in much of the rest of the world and throughout history, these rites are performed by the family and those close to the deceased. To carry out these duties means close contact with the dead body and exposure to strong cues that the deceased individual is actually gone.

While many aspects of funerary rites develop as an outgrowth of the local culture, loved ones engaging in close contact with the body of the deceased is mostly universal. In a survey of the ethnographic literature, Claire White found that the deceased's kin had at least moderately intimate contact with the corpse in approximately 90 percent of cultures with available information about funerary rites.

This contact typically included rituals such as washing, dressing, and prepping the body. The researchers argue that this universal aspect of a culturally varied practice is evidence of it serving a specific psychological function. Intimate contact with a deceased loved one can help shepherd the family through the grieving process by providing veridical cues of death.

In humans, funerary rites have many functions. One understudied function might be to facilitate the flipping of the living/dead switch in our minds. By promoting intimate contact with the corpse and providing reminders that the loved one has passed (such as a funeral service, headstone, or family members expressing their sorrow), funerary rites help reinforce the reality that a loved one is no longer in our social life. Our primate cousins don't have funerals, and they must rely on nonritualized cues to help them recognize and move on from the death of a group member. Without death-related cultural artifacts and rituals, many nonhuman primates rely heavily on strong cues of death, namely, bodily injuries. Some of the clearest evidence for this comes from how primate mothers deal with the death of infants.

Primate infants are prime targets for predators. To help ensure they grow up safely, infants are strongly attached to their mothers. During longer journeys, infants will often ride on their mother's back for added protection. If a chimpanzee troop is ready to move when an infant is sleeping, the mother chimp will pick the infant up and place it on her back; it's sort of like carrying your sleeping child from your car to inside your home. If chimp mothers did not have this instinct, infants would be at risk of being left behind.

As was the case for most of human history, infant mortality in primate populations is quite high. Infants face risk of death from predators, hostile adult males, accidental falls, and diseases, among several other dangers. It isn't uncommon for a primate mother to lose an infant in her lifetime. When an infant primate dies, the mother sometimes responds in a very bizarre fashion: She carries her dead infant for an extended period of time.

Infant corpse carrying is one of the most commonly observed thanatological behaviors (behaviors related to death or dying) in nonhuman primates. It has been recorded in a number of different species, including gorillas, macaques, chimpanzees, bonobos, lemurs, baboons, and several others. Sometimes the mother carries the dead infant for only a few hours, but the behavior has been observed for several days or even weeks. The high frequency of observed instances of infant corpse carrying is likely due to the high rate of infant mortality in nonhuman primates combined with primate mothers' strong instinct to care for their infants. Of course, that instinct should apply only to living infants.

Scientists are still unsure why infant corpse carrying occurs, but there are some clues that suggest the mothers may not have fully grasped the death of their infant. Primate mothers will sometimes engage in other behaviors like grooming or swatting flies away from the deceased infant that imply she is caring for it as if it were alive. It's also not entirely clear why the timing varies so drastically. Why do some mothers never carry their deceased infants while others carry them for several days or weeks?

One factor that seems to influence how long a dead infant is carried by its mother is the context surrounding the death. In a systematic analysis of infant corpse carrying across fifty primate species, researchers found that infants that died by non-gruesome causes, such as stillbirth or illness, were carried for longer periods of time than those that died by more traumatic means, such as electrocution, mishandling, or aggression. The researchers argue that severe bodily injuries provide mothers with clearer cues of death, helping to flip the sticky cognitive switch between life and death.

Death is difficult to identify from motion alone, and before modern medicine, it was even less clear. For other animals without a conception of death, the problem is even more complicated. However, natural selection has found a solution to this problem through curiosity about bodily injuries. Because severe bodily injuries correlate strongly with death, our morbid curiosity about them helps ensure that we don't mistake a dead person as alive or vice versa.

Some of you may be thinking, "Sure, we should be curious about bodily injuries, but not *too* curious. Aren't bodily injuries and corpses disease-ridden and potentially dangerous? Isn't that why we feel disgust toward them?"

Maybe not. The disgust you feel toward a corpse may just be your body warning you not to eat it, and your empathy might be to blame for your feeling of disgust toward some injuries.

CLEAN CORPSES

Disgust evolved as a defense against pathogens. Cues of pathogens, like coughing, putrescent smell, or open sores, signal to our mind that we should initiate behavioral precautions to prevent infection. We gag, get a sick feeling in our stomach, or leave the room when we feel disgust, because those measures help prevent potential sources of pathogenic material from being ingested or otherwise coming into contact with us. Just as we have a physiological immune system that fights off infections inside of our body, we also have a behavioral immune system that helps us take steps to prevent infection in the first place.

Corpses can be pathogenic if the person died from a pathogen. However, many pathogens that kill a host don't survive long after the host dies. The decomposition process does breed some bacteria that can be harmful to eat and produces a putrid smell, which can cause us to gag and motivate us to avoid the decomposing flesh. The gagging response in these situations likely evolved due to the fact that humans eat meat but didn't have great ways of preserving it for most of history. Unlike scavenging animals, humans don't have specialized stomach acid, enzymes, or immune systems that can efficiently deal with the toxins produced by microbes that colonize rotting corpses. Instead, humans usually avoid rotting meat with the help of the disgust response.

Corpses can be toxic to eat without proper preparation, but unless a small subset of diseases such as Ebola or cholera caused the death, fresh corpses aren't that pathogenic to be around. In the West, much of this notion of pathogenic corpses came from the idea that many diseases were caused by miasma, or "bad air." This theory, which predates the germ theory of disease, was rooted in the connection between unsanitary conditions and foul smells. Because these two features often co-occurred in crowded cities, early physicians believed that the putrid smells actually caused bad air, which led to disease. As corpses decayed, they began to emit a putrid smell that was believed to cause disease. The disgust response to the smell was simply telling us not to *eat* the dead, but our culture expanded that to prohibit all contact with the dead.

PAINFULLY DISGUSTING

Have you ever seen someone break a bone? Maybe they fell off a bike or took a nasty leg kick in an MMA match. Think back to a time you saw something like this, even if it was a video. How did you react? You might have made a facial expression and recoiled. Perhaps you looked away and made an audible "ugh" sound. This reaction is similar to the disgust reaction, but what you felt likely wasn't disgust. What you were feeling was probably vicarious pain emanating from the empathy you had for the poor soul who broke their leg.

The icky feeling we get when we see bodily injuries is often described as a feeling of disgust, but some researchers argue that it may not be the emotion of disgust in every case. If a wound is produced by an infectious agent, then the wound is, of course, infectious. We should feel disgust toward that, as it serves as a preventative measure that lowers our chances of coming into contact with an infectious agent. But a cut on a leg that resulted from a fall? That wasn't caused by an infectious agent and isn't infectious. Yet, many people report feeling disgust when they see a noninfectious bodily injury like a cut. One explanation for this is that our perception is wired to be on a hair trigger for cues of disgust. So, the response might fire at *any* type of injury, regardless of whether it's pathogenic in nature. Another explanation is that we simply don't talk about empathic pain as a response, so we code it as disgust in language. If this is true, could our minds actually be able to distinguish infectious injuries from other bodily injuries?

Psychologist Tom Kupfer conducted a series of studies about empathy, disgust, and bodily injuries to test this very question. In his first study, Kupfer generated a list of scenarios that included pathogenic injuries ("sitting next to someone who has red sores on their arm") as well as noninfectious bodily injuries ("seeing a person's hand crushed in a machine"). He then asked participants how disgusted they felt by each scenario. Participants reported feeling disgusted by all the bodily injury scenarios, but their reports of disgust toward noninfectious bodily injuries clustered in ways that separated them from reports of disgust on pathogenic wounds.

The follow-up study to this finding included a creative behavioral task. Kupfer printed out images of injuries, some of which were infectious (e.g., a growth on someone's eye) and some of which were not infectious (e.g., a fishhook caught in someone's eye). He then asked people how disgusted they felt by each image. As previous studies had found, the average disgust rating for an infectious injury was no different from the average disgust rating for a noninfectious injury. In other words, people reported that they felt about as disgusted by the noninfectious injury photos as they did by the infectious injury photos.

Next came the fun part. Kupfer placed the images next to yellow medical waste bags in his lab. Inside of each bag was a bandage that appeared to have been used as medical dressing, appropriately sized for the corresponding injury. On the counter next to the bags were two containers labeled "Biohazard, medical waste." When a participant arrived at the lab, they were instructed to put on a pair of medical gloves and shown a fake document from the hospital where the (ostensibly) used bandages and photographs were from.

Over the course of eight rounds, participants were presented with two bags and two photographs: one with a noninfectious injury and one with an infectious injury. They were asked to inspect each photograph and told that the bag behind the photograph contained the bandage from that injury. Finally, participants were asked to choose which medical dressing they would be more comfortable touching. Participants made their choice and then reached into the medical waste bag to touch the bandage.

Which would you choose to touch, the bandage from a pus-filled sore on someone's eye, or the bandage from someone's eye who had a fishhook stuck through it? If we take the disgust ratings at face value, then we should expect the choice to be evenly split between the two. Of course, this wasn't the case.

Participants in the study overwhelmingly chose to touch the medical dressings that were from the noninfectious injuries; four out of every five avoided the bandages from the infectious injuries. Despite participants reporting similar levels of disgust when shown the photos, there was a clear behavioral difference in which type of injury they were willing to touch. The participants largely avoided the medical dressing used in infectious injuries, but they still reported similar levels of disgust when viewing the noninfectious injuries.

Kupfer suggests that this difference may come down to language. Participants in studies on disgust are usually asked only about their feelings of disgust; that's the only relevant word they're given to express how they feel about an injury. Moreover, the English language doesn't really have a common word for "feelings of vicarious pain due to empathic responding." It's possible that this experience feels akin to disgust, so participants simply call it disgust.

When Kupfer gave the participants more freedom to describe their feelings in response to these injuries, differences between infectious and noninfectious injuries began to emerge. When talking about how they felt when they saw the noninfectious injuries, participants were more likely to mention feelings of empathy or imagined pain. When looking at the infectious injury images, participants were more likely to mention feelings of sickness and repulsion. In participants' minds and behaviors, infectious injuries were treated differently from noninfectious injuries, despite them both being called "disgusting."

The physiological evidence also backs up this distinction. In a study looking at gastric responses to different kinds of injuries, Amitai Shenhav and Wendy Berry Mendes found that infectious injuries could be clearly distinguished from noninfectious injuries. The researchers used a method called electrogastrography to measure muscle contractions in the stomach. If you've ever gagged at the smell of something, you probably understand why muscle contractions in the stomach are a useful measurement here.

One function of disgust is to physically prohibit the ingestion of contaminated food; this is why the smell of rotting meat or other pathogenic indicators can make you gag and feel sick to your stomach. Despite observing that noninfectious injuries elicited similar facial contractions and levels of self-reported disgust, the researchers found that only exposure to infectious injuries caused changes in stomach muscle contractions. Both our minds and our bodies clearly distinguish infectious injuries from noninfectious injuries, even if our language doesn't.

This may also explain a peculiar finding in my own research. The conventional understanding of disgust would suggest that those who possess high trait levels of contamination disgust (i.e., are more likely to experience disgust toward cues of contamination) should not be curious about bodily injuries. The disgust they experience should counteract any curiosity they might feel. But this isn't the case. In my studies, I haven't found an association between disgust sensitivity to contamination and trait levels of morbid curiosity about bodily injuries. Presumably, this is because many bodily injuries are not the result of an infection, so variations in baseline levels of disgust aren't that relevant.

It's important for us to be able to distinguish between a pathogenic injury around which we should express caution and a non-pathogenic injury that is safe for us to help treat. This gives us another purpose for our curiosity about bodily injuries: Morbid curiosity motivates us to gather information about bodily injuries because this information is critical for identifying whether or not we should avoid interacting with the injury.

THE MANY FACETS OF INJURY FASCINATION

Over two thousand years ago, Plato told the story of a man named Leontius. One day, Leontius was walking near the city walls of Piraeus, when he caught a glimpse of an executioner standing over a pile of dead bodies. Leontius felt an overwhelming desire to look at the bodies while simultaneously loathing the thought of them. His morbid curiosity eventually won out and he rushed up to the bodies, shouting at his own eyes, "There! You wretches! Gaze your fill at the beautiful spectacle!"

Leontius felt that one part of his mind had rebelled against him, almost forcing him to confront the mangled bodies. He didn't delight in the sight nor did he plan his trip to the wall so that he might happen upon the executioner's work. He didn't run to see them with joyous excitement. Instead, Leontius fought in vain against the urge to look and, ultimately, lost. His curiosity was too strong, overpowering the other aspects of his mind that might have kept him from looking.

Plato's point in the story of Leontius was to demonstrate the struggle humans can experience between rationality and emotions. However, I believe the story of Leontius says even more about the experience of morbid curiosity. It's often a conflicting feeling. We feel fascinated and intrigued by a corpse or a bodily injury while at the same time feeling disgust (or perhaps more often, empathy toward pain). The counteracting force of these emotions determines to what extent we will indulge in our morbid curiosity. The feeling of disgust or vicarious pain may drive us away, but the curiosity has us peering from a distance.

Natural selection had to build this intrigue, this curiosity, about injuries as a counterweight to other motivational systems that lead to avoidance. Without it, we would only ever shy away from things that sometimes disturb us. Rotting corpses and severed limbs can provide critical information about our environment. Bodily injuries can also provide us with strong cues of death, helping us navigate what can otherwise be a tricky distinction. Finally, our morbid curiosity about bodily injuries can help us identify whether an injury is infectious or not.

7.

THE DEMONS IN OUR DREAMS

They've promised that dreams can come true—but forgot
to mention that nightmares are dreams, too.

—Oscar Wilde

WHAT'S IN A DREAM?

What was the last dream you remember having? Was it a good dream, or was it a nightmare? If you're anything like me, this is a difficult question to answer. I don't dream often, and when I do, the content of my dream usually escapes me within a few minutes of waking. I have always been a bit jealous of people who have frequent, vivid dreams. It seems like that would be a magical way to spend most nights. Then again, maybe it wouldn't be if those dreams were terrible nightmares where you didn't have much control over what was happening.

Nightmares are uncommon for me, but I have died a few times in my dreams. Usually this happens because I've gotten myself into a bad situation in the dream; I didn't see the clues that something would be dangerous and wound up in the wrong place at the wrong time. The dreams where I die are usually the ones I dwell on after I wake up and the ones I remember the longest.

There's a great deal of variation in what people dream about, how vivid the dreams are, and how likely we are to remember our dreams. But everyone dreams. It's a universal feature of human nature, and cultures around the world have long been fascinated by the purpose of dreams. The historical and ethnographic records speak to this, with a well-documented literature of dream interpretation across cultures. The specifics of how these dreams are interpreted vary, but every culture has ideas on how to think about dreams and what they might mean.

The Old Testament gives an early example of oneiromancy, or the interpretation of dreams to foretell the future. In the Book of Genesis, there is a story about the Pharaoh in Egypt who had two dreams that nobody could interpret. In the first dream, he saw seven ugly, gaunt cows emerging from the Nile and devouring seven sleek, fat cows. The Pharaoh briefly woke up after the bizarre dream but soon fell back asleep. He then had a second dream where seven thin heads of grain sprouted and consumed seven healthy heads of grain. The next morning, the Pharaoh called in all the wise men and magicians he could find, but none could make sense of his strange dreams. However, he was sure that they must hold some significant meaning.

The Pharaoh's cupbearer mentioned that two years prior he had met a man named Joseph in prison. The cupbearer said that Joseph had accurately interpreted his dream as well as the dream of another man who was imprisoned with them. Upon hearing this, the Pharaoh had Joseph brought from the prison to interpret his dreams. After hearing the recounting of the dreams, Joseph told the Pharaoh that his dreams meant there would be seven years of abundance followed by seven years of famine. He advised the Pharaoh to appoint a wise man to oversee food storage for the next seven years. Impressed by Joseph's ability to interpret his dreams, the Pharaoh released him from prison and put him in charge of all the lands of Egypt.

Dreams have also inspired modern cultural and scientific progress. The melody to the Beatles' "Yesterday," often listed as one of the greatest and most frequently covered songs of the twentieth century, reportedly came to Paul McCartney in a dream. When he woke up from the dream, he went straight to the piano to replay it. The structure of the molecule benzene, one of the most widely produced chemicals in the world, was also discovered during a dream. Benzene's molecular structure—a ring formed by six hydrogen atoms—had long eluded chemists. One day, after a long series of conference talks, August Kekulé dreamt of a snake devouring its own tail, forming a ringlike shape. When he woke up, Kekulé immediately understood what the dream was about, and the ringlike structure of benzene was suddenly crystal clear to him.

The Western horror genre also has its roots in a dream. In 1815, the Tambora volcano in Indonesia erupted in such a spectacular fashion that it altered the weather across the world for several years. The summer days of 1816 were so frequently filled with booming storm clouds and cooler temperatures that it became known as "the year without a summer." Fortunately for the horror genre, the inclement weather from this eruption trapped Mary and Percy Shelley, Lord Byron, and their companions inside a Swiss vacation house. To fill their time, Lord Byron suggested the group have a competition to see who could write the best ghost story. After no sparks of inspiration for a few days, Mary Shelley had a terrible "waking dream"—the kind of dream that you have just as you're drifting off to sleep. She dreamt of a man who had reanimated a corpse: the inspiration for her greatest novel, *Frankenstein*.

Centuries after Shelley's nightmare, dreams are still inspiring tales of terror. The 2012 supernatural horror movie *Sinister* tells the story of a true crime writer who moves into a big, creepy house and finds a box of what appear to be snuff films that portray actual murders. *Sinister* is a terrifying movie, even taking the top spot in a "scariest movies" study conducted in 2020. C. Robert Cargill, who wrote the script, said in an interview that the movie was inspired by a nightmare he had. In the nightmare, Cargill found an old box of Super 8 film in his attic. When he played the film in his nightmare, he saw a version of what is now the opening shot of *Sinister*.

Scientists are still unsure how dreams occur or why they exist in the first place. One theory is that dreaming occurs due to random neurons firing during sleep. However, it is unlikely that entirely random neuronal firing during sleep would result in coherent audiovisual experiences, no matter how bizarre they might be. Sure, the plots of most dreams look like they've been directed by David Lynch, but they *do* appear to be directed. Even if the story and the characters are a bit odd, the events and characters in dreams are usually recognizable as things that exist or could exist in the world.

The worlds of dreams might be weird, but they are somewhat structured and arise from complex neuronal processes. When complexity coupled with the appearance of specific structure exists in nature, it's usually a good idea to consider why it's there; complex structures are often evolution's maker's mark. One intriguing theory about the evolution of dreaming is that the first dreams were nightmares, and these nightmares encouraged people to prepare for potential dangers in their environment. In other words, our capacity for dreaming may have sprung out of our ancestors' morbid curiosity.

THE TERRIFYING EVOLUTION OF DREAMS

Finnish neuroscientist and philosopher Antti Revonsuo has developed what he calls the threat simulation theory of dreaming. His theory posits that a key function of dreaming is to run simulations of threatening scenarios. These simulations allow our brains to rehearse threat recognition and avoidance behaviors while we sleep, improving our responses to real threats when we are awake. Just like play can be used to simulate dangerous scenarios, dreams can act as threat simulators.

This isn't to say that dreams act *only* as threat simulators. That's obviously not true. People have all sorts of dreams that have nothing to do with threats. Revonsuo's argument is simply that the *ability* to dream, the specific neurological wiring that it requires, evolved due to the adaptive benefits that threat simulation would have. Because we also pay more attention to and are more likely to share information about threats, we are also more inclined to share and listen to stories about threats in our dreams.

It's not easy to study dreams, but the threat simulation theory has managed to rack up quite a bit of evidence in its favor. Although we dream about many different topics, threats make frequent appearances in our dreams. A dream doesn't have to be a terrifying nightmare to include a threat. Aggression, failures, accidents, and other kinds of threats or misfortunes are all common features of dreams. Dreams with high threat content, such as nightmares, are more likely to be remembered vividly after waking up. This might allow the threat-related scenarios to be not only implicitly rehearsed but also consciously reflected upon after waking up and shared with others. Just as our morbid curiosity draws us to horror movies and bad news, so too does it lead us to be fascinated with nightmares.

One prediction of the threat simulation theory is that when threats become apparent in the waking world, they will activate the mind's threat management system. When active, this system will monitor the environment for threats and cause us to simulate potential threats as a rehearsal for what to do if they are encountered. These simulations often happen in the waking world through experiences such as rumination, but they can also occur in the dreaming world. For example, children who have experienced trauma are more than twice as likely to experience threats in their dreams. These dream threats are also more likely to be physically aggressive and pose a threat to the individual in their dream. Increased daily stress, which can activate the threat management system and lead to increased daily threat perception, also predicts greater instances of nightmares. Relatedly, people who have greater baseline vigilance toward threats, like chronically anxious people, report a higher frequency of threats in dreams. Interestingly, anxious people are also more likely to score high in morbid curiosity and seek out threatening entertainment in waking life. More on that in chapter 10.

As is the case with a lot of psychology research, what we know about dreaming comes largely from studies with participants who live in the Western world, mostly Europe and the US. However, there's also some evidence for the threat simulation theory of dreaming from more traditional societies. The Mehinaku people of central Brazil believe that the dreaming world is a real world filled with monsters, spirits, and the dreaming souls of other Mehinaku. They place great importance on the power of dreams as predictors of injury, illness, and death. Because of this, it is a cultural practice of the Mehinaku to recount their dreams to friends and family each morning. This makes them the perfect participants for a study on dream content.

Anthropologist Thomas Gregor collected information about nearly four hundred dreams from the Mehinaku. One intriguing finding from Gregor's study was the frequency and content of aggressive dreams. The Mehinaku had more frequent threatening and aggressive dreams than a comparative sample of Americans. In their dreams, the Mehinaku were typically attacked by other men or dangerous creatures such as jaguars, dogs, snakes, and venomous insects. The aggressors in the Mehinaku dreams are the same types of aggressors or threats they would encounter in the waking world. Unlike the Mehinaku, Americans aren't usually at risk of being injured by dangerous animals in their daily life. This difference shows up in their dreams as well: Animal aggressors are much less common in Americans' dreams.

Some differences in dream threats also emerged between Mehinaku men and women. While women reported more fear and anxiety in response to dangerous animals such as jaguars and wild pigs, men reported greater fear and anxiety in dreams about venomous insects and snakes. Gregor took note of this difference and suggested that in their dreams, Mehinaku men and women each fear the kinds of animals they have little defense against in the waking world. Mehinaku women do not carry weapons and have less experience dealing with large predators. This isn't as much of an issue with Mehinaku men, who carry weapons and are more experienced in dealing with large, dangerous animals. However, strength and hunting ability offer little defense against the venomous insects and snakes that lurk in the bushes and haunt the dreams of Mehinaku men.

The threats that the Mehinaku face in their dreams tend to be those that they are likely to encounter and less equipped to overcome. This is right in line with what Revonsuo argues is the function of dreaming: to simulate threats as a form of mental rehearsal. Ecologically recurrent threats, such as dangerous men, snakes, and large carnivores, made frequent appearances in the Mehinaku dreams.

Experiencing danger in your life increases the frequency of threats in your dreams. Several studies with combat veterans and children exposed to traumatic, life-threatening experiences show that the frequency of nightmares and threatening situations in dreams is abnormally high in these populations. However, even less serious instances of daily danger are associated with increased frequency of threats in dreams.

David Samson of the Sleep and Human Evolution Lab at the University of Toronto has studied dreams in a variety of populations, including small-scale forager societies (the Hadza of Tanzania and the BaYaka of the Democratic Republic of the Congo), Western college students, European adults, individuals diagnosed with nightmare disorder, and individuals diagnosed with social anxiety disorder. His research shows that populations with greater daily instances of life-threatening danger (e.g., the Hadza and Ba-Yaka) also have higher levels of threat dream content. As with the Mehinaku, the threats in the Hadza and BaYaka dreams are often those that these populations are likely to encounter, namely, dangerous animals and hostile men.

Despite the high levels of dream threat content, the Hadza and BaYaka report low levels of negative emotions associated with their dreams compared to Western populations. Samson's research suggests that one reason for this is because the Hadza and BaYaka are more likely to experience resolution and subsequent fear extinction in their dreams. Although they faced hordes of hungry predators and angry groups of enemies in their dreams, these individuals usually found a way to overcome the challenge. In contrast to the forager sample, participants diagnosed with nightmare disorder faced less threat content in dreams but greater negative emotions associated with those threats. In other words, it's not threats in dreams per se that are bad; in fact, those might be good, helping us implicitly learn to regulate negative emotions in the face of fear. As we'll see in chapter 10, this same principle applies to the threats we face in the fictional worlds of horror media.

BUILDING A GOOD THREAT-LEARNING SYSTEM

Unlike many species that inhabit specific environmental niches, humans are well adapted to exploiting new environments. Humans can survive in the dry, sandy deserts of Saudi Arabia, the cold, ruthless tundra of Siberia, the lush forests of the Amazon, the wilds of the Australian Outback, and the high-altitude mountains of Tibet. This migratory nature means that humans, at least in the past several hundred thousand years, have not had a primary predator or environmental danger. Rather, we've had to quickly react and deal with new dangers that we find in varying environments.

The things we more easily learn to fear often have features in common that help our minds process the information as important. For example, humans seem to have a tendency to pay close attention to sharp, angular shapes, possibly because sharp claws and angular teeth are evolutionarily recurrent features of predators. We aren't hardwired to fear lions or wolves specifically but instead to attend to and process features that are shared among predators like lions and wolves. Recurrent features of predators such as sharp teeth and sharp claws draw our attention, allowing us to more efficiently learn about the creatures that possess them.

This is true not just for threatening stimuli but for virtually anything humans learn about. Language is a good example. Humans are not hardwired to learn a *specific language*, but we are hardwired to learn language. We have evolved a predisposition to pay attention to certain linguistic cues and parse information in a way that allows for language learning. Likewise, we have evolved a disposition to pay attention to recurrent cues of threats and efficiently parse information about those threats.

Feature-based learning mechanisms like this are a powerful way to build a threat-learning system because of the ability to quickly learn about things that are likely to be threatening, even if that specific danger has never been encountered. This allows us to be efficient learners even if the threat is entirely new to us, assuming it triggers some of those evolved trip wires. Novelty itself is also an attractor of attention, so when new threats make an appearance, their novelty will also make them stronger attractors of attention and learning. If Revonsuo's threat simulation theory of dreaming is correct, then novel threats that share features with more common threats and that we are not well equipped to handle should make a strong appearance in our dreams. For better or worse, the state of the world in 2020 produced pretty good conditions to test this.

The early months of the COVID-19 pandemic saw a sharp increase in nightmares, and many of these nightmares were pandemic themed. Although themes like being chased or experiencing aggression were still common, people were now having nightmares about things like disease management, isolation, and sickness. Those who were more stressed about the pandemic also reported more threat-related and pandemic-specific dreams.

Just as the ecologically relevant threat of jaguars and snakes filled the dreams of the Mehinaku, dreams of lockdowns and sickness were terrorizing Americans in 2020. Disease is a potent evolutionary pressure in humans, and we've evolved to be sensitive to cues of disease, such as coughing, sneezing, or skin lesions. When our waking world was filled with cues of disease, our minds raced to rehearse threatening disease-related encounters. We consumed pandemic-themed movies, avidly followed COVID-related news, and dreamed of all the terrible possibilities that we might encounter.

DREAMING OF POSSIBILITIES

Like most felines, my cat likes to spend a huge portion of his day napping. It's not uncommon for him to move his paws or twitch his face while sleeping. I assume he's having some sort of cat dream where he's chasing mice or being chased by dogs. However, he's been an indoor cat his entire life, so I'm certain he's never actually experienced either of those things. Of course, I can't ask him about his dreams, and I can't even be sure if he experiences dreams in the same way humans do. However, he does seem to be experiencing *something*, and sometimes those experiences appear pretty clear. There have been a few times when he has jolted awake, pounced several feet in the air, and stood frozen with a look of terror and confusion when he landed. Was he having a cat nightmare?

There's good reason to believe that many animals do experience dreams in some fashion. Some of this comes from behaviors like those I've witnessed in my cat. Other, more scientific, evidence comes from measuring neural oscillations, or "brain waves," in sleeping animals. Neurons in the brain communicate using electrical signals, allowing scientists to measure the rhythmic patterns of brain waves that are produced by these electrical signals when certain behaviors take place.

In many animals, the hippocampal theta wave is associated with predatory behaviors and other responses elicited from survival-related information in the environment. Interestingly, the hippocampal theta wave is also active in animals during REM sleep—the part of the sleep cycle when dreams occur most frequently and most vividly in humans. Because REM sleep is defined physiologically by specific brain waves, muscle atonia, and the eponymous rapid eye movements, we can measure whether or not it exists in other animals. We can then see what other areas of the brain are active and what aspects of behavior are present during REM sleep. With this technique, there's no need for the cats to recount to us their dreams.

Physiological malfunctions that cause you to wake up during REM sleep lend some insight into what is happening during this time. Waking up during REM sleep can lead to an absolutely terrifying experience known as sleep paralysis. Sleep paralysis is terrifying in part because you wake up and find yourself unable to move. The fear of having been paralyzed somehow during your sleep washes over you as you lie in bed unable to move anything other than your anxious eyes. As nerve-wracking as this can be, waking up paralyzed is only the second-most frightening thing about sleep paralysis.

The far more terrifying aspect of sleep paralysis is the hallucinations that often accompany it. And as luck would have it, you almost never hallucinate about anything good. During REM sleep, the amygdala is highly active. If you recall from chapter 2, the amygdala plays an important role in threat perception. When you wake up paralyzed in a dark room with your amygdala firing on all cylinders, your mind is working overtime to figure out where the threat is. Much like with extreme anxiety, the amygdala is telling the rest of your brain to be aware of impending danger.

Because there are no threats around and your mind is still in the highly imaginative state of REM sleep, you begin to hallucinate threats. It's like a terrible drug trip where you are pinned to your bed by the weight of the world. Sleep paralysis hallucinations often involve horrible creatures or ominous beings that lurk in the corners of your room. These unwelcome visitors are accompanied by heightened feelings of fear and impending doom from your overactive amygdala. I've experienced sleep paralysis only once, and it was truly one of the most terrifying experiences of my life. I have no idea what kind of entity I was simulating, but the demon-looking creature in the corner of my room was something straight out of the darkest of horror films.

Another disorder that lends insight into what goes on during REM sleep occurs when you are asleep during REM but able to move. In humans, this can lead to disorders like sleepwalking; the body moves about as usual while the conscious parts of the mind are in sleep mode. In animal models, it is possible to disable the neurons that keep the body from moving during REM sleep. This has led to some fascinating clues about the nature of dreaming in other animals. If the neurons that keep the body paralyzed in REM sleep are disabled, many animals will act out full behavioral repertoires in their sleep, similar to humans who have sleep disorders. For example, one group of researchers disabled these neurons in cats and found that the cats would rise up in their sleep and attack or defend themselves. Presumably, those cats were having the same kinds of dreams—or nightmares—that my cat sometimes has.

Maybe the cats in those early studies had experienced being chased by a dog and they were acting that out in their dreams. However, I'm sure my cat has never been chased by a dog (or by anything remotely threatening, for that matter). Is it possible that my cat was having a nightmare about an entirely novel threat when he woke up with a look of fear on his face? Although it isn't definitive, some studies have suggested that animals can dream about things they have never experienced. One of the cleverest techniques for demonstrating this was developed by neuroscientist Freyja Ólafsdóttir and her colleagues.

Ólafsdóttir fitted rats with electrode helmets that allowed her to continuously record neuronal activity. She had the rats explore a T-shaped tunnel where each side wing of the tunnel was blocked by a transparent wall. The rats could see down the wings of the tunnel but could not go inside them. In one wing of the tunnel, there was a snack—a reward for the rat. After this experience, the rats went back to their home cage and slept, still wearing their electrode helmets.

The next day, the rats were allowed to fully explore the left and right wings of the tunnel while wearing their electrode helmets. Now the researchers had information on (1) which neurons fired when the rats were only able to look down a wing of the tunnel, (2) which neurons fired when the rats were asleep after that experience, and (3) which neurons fired when they were able to explore the formerly blocked wings of the tunnel the next day. Incredibly, the researchers found that the neurons that fired when the rats were able to actually explore the formerly blocked wing of the tunnel were also firing in the rats' sleep *the night before*. In their dreams, the rats seemed to be simulating an exploration of places that they hadn't yet been.

The fact that these rats seemed to have been dreaming about something they'd never physically experienced is remarkable. It suggests that animals might in fact simulate experiences, and these experiences are sometimes relevant to their survival. It also suggests that coherent dreams might be quite old from an evolutionary perspective. If it's present in rats and cats, it is likely that it was also present in their last common ancestor, which would have lived tens of or perhaps even a hundred million years ago.

If dreaming originally evolved to simulate threats, then nightmares could be considered one of the oldest forms of morbid curiosity. By dreaming up dangerous predators and enacting the full suite of physiological actions associated with encountering them, animals can implicitly learn about and rehearse interactions with threats. Through dreaming, natural selection may have found a crafty way to help prey rehearse interactions with predators long before higher cognition evolved. In fact, it may have done this more than once in history.

From an evolutionary standpoint, you don't have much in common with an octopus. The last common ancestor between humans and octopuses existed over half a *billion* years ago, before the divergence between vertebrates and invertebrates. You are more closely related to a dinosaur than you are to an octopus. And yet, despite the octopus being one of our most distant biological cousins, we both dream of threats.

Octopuses appear to have a REM-like sleep state called active sleep. During active sleep, the octopus will display wake-like behaviors and neural signatures, suggesting it is experiencing a qualitatively different stage of sleep. Occasionally, the octopus will thrash about, change its skin color, and even shoot ink: all behaviors that it enacts when facing a threat. As with dreaming in mammals, the intact and coherent physiological changes suggest that the octopus is simulating an embodied experience—an activity that might reap many of the same benefits as waking simulations such as play.

The ability to dream about situations you've never actually experienced is a powerful way to rehearse threats. If you have to wait until you've experienced a threat to dream about it, then dreaming is a bit less useful in prevention. However, if dreams can be proactive, then the threat simulation theory becomes even more plausible, and the evolutionary benefits of nightmares become clear. My cat may very well have been dreaming about being chased by a dog, even though he's never actually been chased by one. Perhaps he will now be better equipped to escape a chase with a dog if he ever found himself in one.

8.

THE DARK EMPATH

Compassion is knowing our darkness well enough that
we can sit in the dark with others.

—*Pema Chödrön*

PULLING AT THE THREAD OF EMPATHY

The science of horror is a small field. There aren't many people studying horror fans or morbid curiosity, so I'm always kept abreast of new developments and ongoing projects. In fact, most of that research happens at the Recreational Fear Lab, where I work as a behavioral scientist.

Because it's a small field, there are still *a lot* of open questions. One of the most common questions I get when I talk to people about horror is whether horror fans are simply less empathetic than other people. People who are not horror fans have this question (or more often, this assumption) because they don't understand how some people can not only watch but also *enjoy* a genre with themes of suffering, violence, and fear. They must lack empathy, right? After all, just look at the stuff they're interested in!

So what exactly does science say when it comes to horror, morbid curiosity, and empathy? Is low empathy a necessary condition for someone to have an interest in the macabre?

I dug deep into the scientific literature on this topic several years ago to see what I could learn. I found a few studies and several popular-science articles proclaiming that horror fans had low empathy. However, many of these studies were simply citing other studies when they made the claim about low empathy. When I looked at where they were getting this information, I found that nearly all the studies and popular-science articles were citing the same original study: a 2005 meta-analysis on the enjoyment of mediated fright and violence.

A meta-analysis is a study that looks at results from all previous studies on a given topic and systematically synthesizes them. Because they quantify and summarize results from previous studies, meta-analyses are considered the gold standard when it comes to scientific knowledge. However, a strong meta-analysis is dependent upon many good-quality studies and consistently defined variables. When you have only a few studies or when the variables are inconsistently defined, the results may not be reliable. If you have several studies but many of them suffer methodological issues, then you are just summarizing questionable findings.

This meta-analysis looked at variables related to what the authors called mediated fright and violence, which is a fancy term for scary entertainment. One of the many variables they analyzed was empathy (or more specifically, empathic concern). A cursory look at the paper would indeed leave the reader with the impression that horror fans have low empathy. In the abstract, the authors state that their results confirm that people with low empathy are more likely to find enjoyment in the horror genre. It seems like an open-and-shut case. However, a closer look at the results reveals that the story is not so straightforward. After digging deeper into the results, there were three red flags that caught my attention.

The first red flag was the number of studies. While there technically isn't a minimum number of studies required for a meta-analysis, the more studies the better. Only *six studies* measured empathic concern in relation to enjoyment of horror, a small number for a meta-analysis. I don't fault the authors for this—there hasn't been much research on horror fandom and empathy. It also seems intuitive that horror fans would be low in empathy. After all, how could an empathetic person enjoy a genre with so much pain and suffering? Of course, our intuitions about human behavior are often the aspects of psychology that we should scrutinize most heavily. When we do, we sometimes find that our intuition doesn't capture the phenomenon as well as we expected.

The second red flag was the samples that were used in the studies. The meta-analysis covered only a small demographic range, with samples consisting of either high school teenagers or undergraduate students in the US. We have to be careful about extending findings from US college students to people of all age ranges or even people of the same age who aren't in college. I suspect many of you reading this book are horror fans and are neither high school teens nor college students.

The final red flag was the one that moved me from "Maybe this finding is true in a narrow sense" to "We really have no idea how empathy is related to enjoyment of the horror genre." Of the six studies that measured empathic concern, only *one* demonstrated a fairly strong correlation. Another exhibited a small to moderate correlation, and the remaining four studies showed very small and insignificant correlations between enjoyment of horror and empathic concern.

As it turns out, the authors noticed something interesting about the two studies that showed a meaningful correlation between empathy and horror enjoyment. One of those studies used a film clip featuring torture and extreme violence while the other showed a movie scene that portrayed a brutal murder without any sort of resolution. In the case of these two studies, the construct being measured wasn't really enjoyment of horror movies per se. Rather, it was something closer to enjoyment of seeing victimization. It would be like showing a bunch of people a tragic breakup scene from a rom-com and then asking them how much they enjoyed it. The results probably wouldn't tell us much about the psychology of rom-com fans, but they might tell us something about the psychology of sadists.

When those two studies were removed from the analysis, the association between empathic concern and enjoyment of horror vanished with them. In other words, the meta-analysis couldn't really say *anything* about the association between empathy and enjoyment of horror. Unfortunately, this caveat wasn't featured in the abstract, and readers who casually read the meta-analysis would come away believing that the science says that those who enjoy horror have less empathy.

This meta-analysis has been referenced numerous times, both in academic articles and in the popular press, to support the idea that horror fans lack empathy. At the time I am writing this, the paper has been cited by more than three hundred other scientific papers.

Because people often cite meta-analyses as authoritative support for a finding, it's had a huge influence on how the scientific community and the public view the relationship between empathy and horror enjoyment. However, a close reading of this meta-analysis would bring you to the realization that the argument that horror fans lack empathy holds very little water.

TESTING THE STEREOTYPE

The erroneous conclusion from the meta-analysis aligned with what appeared to be a common preconceived notion that horror fans lack empathy. But did people really stereotype horror fans as cold and heartless monsters? I decided to test this hypothesis myself. To do this, I created a set of random user profiles that displayed a name, gender, age, and favorite movie genre. An example of one of the profiles might look like this:

> **Name:** Ben
> **Gender:** Man
> **Age:** 33
> **Favorite Movie Genre:** Horror

I created hundreds of these profiles and showed them to my study participants. I then asked the participants to predict other traits that the person in the profile might have. I introduced the study as a sort of game so that participants would be incentivized to think carefully about their answers. I told participants that these were profiles of real people who had completed personality questionnaires in another study, and if they accurately predicted the personality of the person in the profile, they would receive a monetary bonus.

Despite my doubts, I was hoping that horror fans wouldn't be perceived as less empathetic or compassionate. After all, I don't want there to be a stigma attached to being a horror fan. However, the data showed what I had predicted: Participants rated horror fans as less empathetic, less compassionate, and less kind than fans of other genres. Lest there be any doubt in the numbers, this assumption showed up in the participants' free responses as well. One participant said, quite bluntly, "I assumed that horror fans might not be kind or compassionate."

This bias was not universal among my participants. Those who chose horror as their favorite genre had rated profiles of horror fans to be just as empathetic and compassionate as fans of other genres. Some of this is likely due to general biases people have for their in-group. However, horror fans also spend a lot more time around other horror fans. Their perceptions are based on real experiences with those people.

A BRIEF DETOUR INTO EMPATHY

Empathy is a notoriously misunderstood and messy topic. It's something that everyone thinks they know quite well but scientists can't seem to agree on. An early account of empathy comes from the eighteenth-century Scottish philosopher and economist Adam

Smith (though he referred to the phenomenon as sympathy). In *The Theory of Moral Sentiments*, Smith describes how humans sympathize with one another by imagining themselves in others' shoes:

> In every passion of which the mind of man is susceptible, the emotions of the bystander always correspond to what, by bringing the case home to himself, he imagines should be the sentiments of the sufferer.

Modern scientific takes on empathy often break it down into two broad types. The first type of empathy is called cognitive empathy. Cognitive empathy corresponds closely with the concept of theory of mind, which is the capacity to represent the mental state of another person. In other words, cognitive empathy refers to the ability to consider and understand another person's thoughts and feelings. This form of empathy is crucial to much of our everyday social life. When our friend tells us about a fun experience they had, we understand that they felt good during it. When we watch a movie, we can cognitively empathize with the protagonist; we take their perspective to better understand why they might have behaved in a certain way or felt the way they did.

The second broad type of empathy is affective empathy. Affective empathy is the more emotional side of empathy. When you engage in affective empathy, you *feel* what the other person is feeling; it's a matching of emotional states with another person. For most people, this process is effortless and can even occur when you don't want it to occur. If we watch a sad movie, our eyes may begin to well up though we're doing our best to choke back the tears. When we see the joy in a loved one's face, we feel joyous even without consciously imagining ourselves in their shoes.

Cognitive and affective empathy are both at play when we engage with a story. Most people don't open a novel and consume it as a list of facts about a situation (and if you do, that might be why you don't like novels). Instead, we open a novel and *it consumes us*. A good story transports us from reading descriptions on a page to mind-wandering hallucinations about a fantasy world. We take this for granted, but it's really an incredible biological feat. With just a few inches of squiggly lines, we can transport ourselves into any possible—or even impossible—situation. We can change our identities, fight terrible beasts, or wield powers that defy the laws of physics. Despite sounding like magic, this doesn't take much effort for most people.

Filmmakers are intuitive experts when it comes to manipulating empathy to fuel a story. By framing close-up shots of a character's face, the filmmaker is encouraging you to take the character's perspective. By forcing your visual attention on a single person and their experience, the filmmaker is making it as easy as possible for you to take the perspective of the character. Despite their (maligned) reputation for encouraging violence and cruelty and discouraging empathy, horror films often make use of the up-close view of the victim's face to encourage the audience to empathize with the victim.

Mathias Clasen gives an example of this from one of the more extreme horror movies, *Hostel*. Released in 2005, *Hostel* is classified by many as "torture porn" for its excessive violence and gore. The movie tells the story of three young men who travel to eastern Europe only to be kidnapped and subjected to torture by the highest bidder. The movie is dark and gruesome; drilling holes in a man who is strapped to a chair is one of the lighter scenes of torture the audience witnesses.

Despite its grisly nature, the camera shots in *Hostel* still encourage its viewers to empathize with the victims. In one of the key scenes in the movie, the camera dials in on the protagonist's facial expressions of pain and fear while he is being tortured. The tight shot framing the victim encourages the audience to take his perspective; the agonizing facial expression of the victim powerfully evokes a shared feeling of fear and pain in the audience.

Some of you might be thinking that these two types of empathy sound pretty similar. And you're right, cognitive and affective empathy are clearly related and work in tandem to produce the larger empathic experience. Still, there's a mound of evidence supporting the claim that these two types of empathy are neurologically separable.

Psychological surveys can also distinguish the two types of empathy. During my deep dive into the scientific literature on empathy, I came across a scale that I thought did an excellent job of capturing both cognitive and affective facets of empathy. The aptly named Questionnaire of Cognitive and Affective Empathy was created to address the lack of psychological measures that directly assess cognitive and affective empathy. It uses items from multiple validated empathy scales in addition to a few new items to tap into the two major components of empathy. To assess cognitive empathy, the scale asks questions that get at one's ability to take the perspective of another person and simulate their experiences. For affective empathy, the questions center around the extent to which another person's emotions and experiences affect your own mental state.

I had evidence that people stereotyped horror fans as generally less empathetic, less compassionate, and less kind. Now I wanted to know if there was any truth in these stereotypes. Are horror fans really the cold, heartless monsters that many people think they are?

COLDHEARTED MONSTERS OR SOFTHEARTED HORROR FANS?

The follow-up study I designed was relatively straightforward. To measure trait levels of empathy, I had participants complete the Questionnaire of Cognitive and Affective Empathy. This would tell me how much cognitive and affective empathy each participant had, much like personality tests tell you how extraverted or agreeable you are. As I'll talk about a bit later, empathy and compassion are not necessarily the same thing, so I also wanted a separate measure of compassion. I chose a measure of coldheartedness from the Psychopathic Personality Inventory to assess compassion—or, in this case, the lack thereof.

The Psychopathic Personality Inventory is an overall measure of psychopathy. Unlike prior measures of psychopathy developed for incarcerated populations, the Psychopathic Personality Inventory was designed to assess trait levels of subclinical psychopathy in the general population. It measures different facets of psychopathy, including fearlessness, rebellious nonconformity, social potency, blame externalization, and coldheartedness. Coldheartedness here refers to a general disregard for the well-being of others. In other words, it's the opposite of compassion.

Now that I had measures of compassion and empathy, I needed to know whether or not people were fans of horror. I thought it would be interesting to look not just at horror broadly but also subgenres within horror. For my purposes, I used a list of horror subgenres from the movie rating website Rotten Tomatoes. The list contained five main subgenres: gore/splatter, killer, monster, paranormal, and psychological. This list also happened to map quite well onto the topics covered by the four domains of morbid curiosity: bodily injuries, minds of dangerous people, violence, and the paranormal.

To make sure everyone had the same "type" of horror movie in mind when rating the subgenres, I gave each subgenre a simple definition and provided a few examples of prototypical movies. *Saw*, for example, is a prototypical gore/splatter film, *Poltergeist* is a prototypical paranormal film, *Halloween* is a prototypical killer film, and so on. At the end of the survey, I also asked the participants to tell me which of those five subgenres was their favorite.

A person's enjoyment of the horror subgenres was mostly unrelated to how empathetic or coldhearted they were. In the few cases where there was an association, it was a *positive* association with empathy and a *negative* association with coldheartedness. In other words, some horror fans were, if anything, *more* empathetic and compassionate (i.e., less coldhearted) than people who didn't like horror.

Those who enjoyed paranormal movies were the real empaths.

Participants who liked paranormal horror films scored higher in multiple facets of cognitive and affective empathy. Enjoyment of paranormal horror was also negatively associated with coldheartedness. This was a particularly intriguing finding since those who claim to be able to interact with the paranormal sometimes call themselves "empaths." According to some, paranormal empaths have a strong understanding of the thoughts and feelings of others around them, which helps them understand and communicate with spirits. It seems they aren't entirely wrong.

Asking people about themselves is one thing, but if I could somehow get a behavioral measure of horror fandom, that would be more convincing. In the first study, I had people compare themselves to others in terms of being a horror fan. However, people may not have a good grasp of how much of a horror fan the average person is, which could skew their answers. Two different participants might both rate themselves as a 4 out of 5 but be very different in the degree to which they actually engage with horror. Their perceptions might be similar, but their behaviors could be quite different.

To account for this, I gave participants a list of fifty popular horror movies and asked them to indicate which ones they had seen in the past ten years. I then gave them the same empathy questionnaire as in the previous study. Replicating my previous study, I found no association between trait levels of empathy and how many horror movies a participant had seen.

I decided to conduct a final study to see how horror fans behaved when they were given the opportunity to act compassionately. I contacted the participants who'd completed my initial survey to test this. I told them that half of the people who participated in the initial study had been randomly drawn to receive a bonus payment, and they were in that half. It was their lucky day (though, in reality, all participants got this message). I also told them that, if they wished to do so, they could donate any percentage of their bonus to a participant whose name was not drawn to receive the bonus. There was no pressure to do so, but if they wished to share in the good fortune, they simply had to tell me how much of their bonus they wanted to anonymously donate to a participant whose name was not drawn.

In economics and psychology, this is known as the dictator game. There are a number of dictator game variations, but they all have the same basic premise: A participant is given a sum of money and told that they may keep all of it or donate any portion of it they wish to another person. There are no repercussions for not donating and no extra benefits for donating. And, if you do donate, the recipient cannot reach out to you to thank you. It is essentially an anonymous donation out of compassion.

I was curious how the horror fans would fare in this compassion test. Would their actions live up to their words?

I was able to get in touch with about two hundred of the participants who'd completed the initial study. Of those, about half decided to donate some portion of their bonus. Horror fans were just as likely as non–horror fans to donate some portion of their bonus to a less fortunate participant. There was also no correlation between the amount donated and how much the donor enjoyed horror. In other words, when it came to behavior, horror fans didn't appear to be any more, or—importantly—any less, compassionate than non–horror fans. You can love *Saw* and still care about people.

The findings from these studies ran counter to previous research and to public perception, but they made perfect sense to me. In order for horror movies to be interesting, horror fans *must* have empathy. When we engage in any kind of fantasy, we use our powers of empathy. A movie is interesting largely because we imagine ourselves in the protagonist's shoes; we empathize with them. When they feel afraid, we feel afraid. When they cringe in pain, we cringe with them. The monster is often front and center in horror, but it's the human protagonists who make horror work. We aren't afraid of the monster just because it's a monster. We are afraid of the monster because it hunts and kills people like us.

Horror plays on our capacity for empathy. We see this in all sorts of horror media, including interactive forms such as haunted houses. I was once discussing empathy and horror fans with Ben Armstrong, co-owner of the famous Netherworld haunt in Georgia. Like many people in the horror community, Ben was not surprised to hear that horror fans score average, or even a bit high, in empathy. He brought up the fact that many haunts use what the folks in the industry call "pleaders." Pleaders are actors who are placed in the haunt at specific locations and plead with visitors for help. They will typically be helpless looking, perhaps trapped in a cage or chained to a wall. As they fight their way through the haunt, visitors have the option to try to free the pleader. Most people are wary, knowing good and well the pleaders are haunt actors who are likely part of a trap. Still, it is difficult for the guests to resist cries of help; the pleaders successfully draw them in by triggering compassion and empathy.

DARK PERSONALITY TRAITS

Historical events have often informed academic thought regarding the darker side of humanity. World War II in particular left its mark on the study of human behavior. The brutal nature of the Holocaust had many scientists asking how it was possible that so many average, everyday Germans found themselves on the wrong side of one of history's most abhorrent events. As a result, many of the classic social psychology experiments that followed World War II focused on how situational factors could produce bad behavior from otherwise normal people. If we could understand how situational contexts influence behavior, we might be able to prevent many of the atrocities we see in the world.

When people commit a terrible act, we want to know why they did it and how they could do something so terrible. Iconic studies in psychology like Stanley Milgram's shock experiment and Philip Zimbardo's Stanford prison experiment focused on the social circumstances that could turn people bad. More recently, psychologists have been asking how individual differences in personality might lead to evil behavior. Situational contexts clearly influence behavior, but could some people be more prone to evil actions by their very nature? Could some people have dark personalities?

The idea that certain traits make up a dark core of personality came about in the early 2000s. In a now hugely influential paper, psychologists Delroy Paulhus and Kevin Williams identified a set of personality traits that they called the "dark triad": narcissism, Machiavellianism, and psychopathy.

The word "narcissism" comes from the Greek mythological figure

Narcissus. Narcissus was a young and beautiful hunter who was, to put it bluntly, obsessed with himself. One day, Narcissus caught a glimpse of his reflection in a pool of water. He was stunned by the sight of himself and became so enamored with the view that he couldn't think about anything else. In fact, he was so infatuated that he spent the rest of his life staring at his own reflection. I'm sure many of you can think of someone like this.

Narcissus embodies what psychologists today call a narcissistic personality. Not all narcissists are the same, though. Psychologists have identified two types of narcissism: grandiose narcissism and vulnerable narcissism. Grandiose narcissism is the more classic and familiar form of narcissism. It's associated with feelings of superiority, egocentric admiration, and a dominant interpersonal style. While still self-centered, vulnerable narcissists don't display these feelings of grandiosity, are highly sensitive to rejection, and frequently experience negative emotions. Grandiose narcissists tend to be more extraverted and socially bold to uphold their self-esteem while vulnerable narcissists tend to be more introverted and avoidant to uphold theirs.

The term "Machiavellianism" comes from the sixteenth-century Italian diplomat and political theorist Niccolò Machiavelli. Machiavelli is famous for his classic book *The Prince*, in which he advises young kings and lords to centralize and hold their power by any means necessary. He argues that deceit, fraud, and even violence can be justified in a leader's pursuit of stabilizing power. To put his philosophy into a memorable phrase, "the ends justify the means."

Some people score high in a personality trait that corresponds with the attitude that Machiavelli encouraged in *The Prince*. Suitably, psychologists have called this trait Machiavellianism. People with high levels of Machiavellianism tend to have a duplicitous interpersonal style. That is, they can be deceitful in order to achieve some personal gain. They will flatter and say the right things if they think it will get them ahead.

Psychopathy is a trait that most of you are probably familiar with in one way or another. The trait has been popularized in movies and TV shows through characters like Dexter Morgan, Hannibal Lecter, and Anton Chigurh. Of course, many of the psychopaths you see on TV are exaggerated versions of real-world psychopaths. The ones on TV are shown to be intelligent, cold, and merciless killers. Although the "cold" and "merciless" descriptors might be accurate, many psychopaths aren't killers, and their intelligence tends to be rather average.

Subclinical psychopathy, which is the kind measured in the dark triad, refers to the everyday variation in psychopathic traits that most people possess. Like other personality traits, subclinical psychopathy varies quite a bit in the population. Those high in subclinical psychopathy often exhibit a fearless dominance in social interactions, little to no anxiety in the face of danger, and a callousness toward people. Those who score high in subclinical psychopathy are not completely devoid of empathy like clinical psychopaths and are not as likely to be antisocial criminals. However, they can be cold and calculating in social situations.

While somewhat distinct, these three personality traits share some core features such as disagreeableness, duplicity, self-promotion, and disregard for the well-being of other people. Everyone has some degree of these traits; we are all a little bit narcissistic, a little bit

Machiavellian, and even a little bit (subclinically) psychopathic. The concern is when an individual has high levels of all three traits.

THE DARK EMPATH

A few years ago I came across a scientific paper with an intriguing finding. The authors were looking at the relationship between empathy and the dark triad. They found four personality profiles in their sample: (1) people who scored average in empathy and low in dark traits (what they called typical), (2) empaths who scored high in empathy and low in the dark triad, (3) traditional dark personalities who scored high in the dark triad and low in empathy, and (4) a newly discovered group of "dark empaths" who scored high in the dark triad and high in empathy.

It may sound obvious that four profiles would show up—after all, there are four possible ways to combine high and low versions of two traits. However, everything in the scientific literature said there should only be three. According to years of research, dark personalities should have a limited capacity for empathy. There shouldn't be a group of people with high dark personality traits and high empathy. Dark empaths shouldn't exist. But, apparently, they do.

After reading the dark empath paper, I emailed the researchers involved. The dark empaths they were describing sounded a lot like the morbidly curious people I had been studying—high in some dark traits, but not low in empathy. The researchers and I decided to work together on a new project looking at morbid curiosity and dark empaths. Our first task was to make sure dark empaths were really a distinct group: Could we find them again in a new sample of participants?

We recruited several hundred people in the US to complete assessments that measured both empathy and dark personality traits. This time, we decided to use a psychological instrument that measures something called the dark tetrad. The dark tetrad is a newer measure of the dark triad that includes sadism as a fourth trait. To measure empathy, we used the same empathy measure that I used in the paper on empathy in horror fans: the Questionnaire of Cognitive and Affective Empathy.

As in the original study, we found two "dark" groups: dark empaths and dark tetrads. The dark empaths were the same group of people my colleagues had found before: people high in dark traits and high in empathy. The dark tetrads were people who were high in dark traits but low in empathy, consistent with the more traditional finding of people who have dark traits. We found that those in both "dark" groups—the dark empaths and dark tetrads—were more likely to be more morbidly curious than the average person. Some degree of darkness was important for morbid curiosity, but empathy (or the lack thereof) wasn't. What could this mean?

I think this finding has two important consequences for how we think about morbidly curious people and dark traits more generally. The first is that empathy seems to have very little to do with one's interest in the macabre. Despite what a few studies in the 1980s suggested, there appears to be no evidence that morbid curiosity requires limited empathy. The second key insight is that dark traits don't necessitate low empathy. This claim was much more controversial. Decades of research has shown that traits like psychopathy, narcissism, and Machiavellianism are associated with low empathy. Some researchers have even argued that low empathy is a core aspect of the dark triad.

Two studies shouldn't sway scientific opinion too much in the face of years of competing evidence. However, it wasn't just two studies; I was beginning to see cracks in the foundation everywhere I looked. In addition to the discovery of the dark empaths, I had also found evidence that horror fans don't seem to lack empathy—in fact, they may even have more empathy in some cases. This was a controversial finding not just because a few studies in the 1980s found the opposite, but also because horror fans consistently scored higher in dark traits, even in my own studies. They scored high in traits that were supposed to be mutually exclusive with high empathy.

Two seemingly contradictory things appear to be true: Horror fans and other morbidly curious people *do* score higher in dark traits, but they do *not* score lower in empathy on average. Morbid curiosity itself seems to have little to do with empathy or compassion.

One possible explanation for this is that we have something wrong when it comes to the concept of dark traits. Perhaps we don't fully understand what it means to have high *subclinical* levels of traits like narcissism and psychopathy. At the clinical level, a psychopath does indeed have empathy deficits. At the subclinical level, this is looking less certain. It might not be the *ability* to empathize that is impaired, but rather that the *involuntary tendency* to empathize is lower. In other words, dark personalities can empathize, but they may often choose not to for one reason or another. Their empathy might be a bit less automatic than other people's empathy.

Another possibility, which is not mutually exclusive with the first, is that we have empathy all wrong.

EMPATHY CAN BE ... BAD?

Empathy is widely seen as a noble virtue that we should cultivate. If only we could get people to be more empathetic, people say, many of our social ills would simply dissolve.

Plenty of scientists have also argued that empathy is the core of our humanity. In his book *The Science of Evil*, psychologist Simon Baron-Cohen makes the claim that the origins of cruelty lie in a lack of empathy. At the heart of evil, Baron-Cohen argues, is a hole where empathy should be. It's an intuitive and catchy claim, but it's incorrect. A lack of empathy is not at the root of cruelty, at least not *all* cruelty. In fact, empathy can sometimes lead to cruelty.

Psychologist Paul Bloom makes the argument that empathy can sometimes be bad in his popular and controversially titled book, *Against Empathy*. The book isn't as one-sided as the title suggests. Bloom talks at length about how empathy works and how incredible it can be when it motivates helping behavior. When we see another person in need, we often feel compelled to help them. When a loved one is hurting, we can literally *feel* their pain. It really is a bit magical. But like all magic, empathy has a dark side.

Back when cable television was common in households, you would often see commercials for humanitarian charities. Many of these charities were for starving children in a faraway country. If you watched these commercials with the critical eye of a psychologist, you'd notice something interesting: The commercials consisted mostly of long, focused shots on a single sad child. These shots were usually followed by an offer to symbolically adopt the child through a monthly donation. By symbolically adopting the child, you might receive monthly updates on them, such as a photo, a story about their week, and specifics on how your donation helped them. The charities really sold the personalization aspect of giving. You were financially adopting a single child, improving their life, and helping alleviate their hardships.

Presumably, a charity helping to feed children is helping to feed hundreds, if not thousands of children. So why do only a few children make it on the commercial? Why not show a group shot of thousands of starving children? If you remember what we learned earlier in the chapter about horror filmmakers and why they focus some shots on victims' faces, you already know the answer.

Focusing on a single child is a great way to hack affective empathy. If I show you a thousand children in need, it doesn't tap as deeply into those evolutionarily old circuits in the brain that allow you to understand another person and motivate you to help them. It's not personal. If I show you one starving kid, those areas of the brain related to empathy light up like fireworks. Helping a thousand kids *should* feel better than helping a single child, but it doesn't. Our brains are wired for helping the few closest to us, which makes empathy a poor moral guide in some cases.

This leads us to the next point: Empathy tends to have a narrow scope. Our empathic spotlight is brightest around our tight-knit social circle and slowly dims as we move out. This effect is probably due to the structure of human social living throughout most of human evolutionary history. For much of our time on the planet, humans lived in small groups, and other groups of humans were not necessarily friendly. In this context, the narrow scope of empathy would have worked quite well to motivate us to help those who are most important to our evolutionary success. In the context of a modern-day, multimillion-person metropolis, this doesn't always work as well. In that environment, empathy has its shortcomings, and it can lead us astray.

If we really want to shine a light on the darker side of empathy, let's consider a torturer. He has his victim tied to a chair with nowhere to go. He has a dozen tools at his disposal, and his job is to make the next hour of his victim's life as miserable as possible. How does he go about doing this? One way would be to randomly select a tool, randomly select a body part, and go to work. Of course, this isn't how torture works, and it probably isn't how you were imagining he would go about it. Another way for him to effectively torture his victim is to empathize with him.

If the torturer really wants to make his victim's life as miserable as possible, then he needs to identify the most painful methods of torture. The simplest way for the torturer to inflict as much pain as possible is to put himself in his victim's shoes—to imagine how painful a particular method would be if he were in the chair. To effectively torture, he needs to engage cognitive tools like perspective taking.

There are other cases where you might think someone would need to engage their empathy, but in fact they don't, and perhaps shouldn't. Let's say you need to go to the hospital for surgery. It's a serious surgery; a heart transplant. The outcome of this surgery—and your life—lies in the hands of the surgeon leading the operation. Now, if I let you pick between two surgeons, one who scored high in empathy and one who scored low in empathy, which would you choose? Perhaps you choose the empathetic surgeon—after all, you want the surgeon to have your best interests in mind. And for that, they should be empathetic, right?

Well, maybe not.

As you lie unconscious on the operating table with medical instruments piercing your body, it's probably best if the surgeon isn't feeling distress from your pain or taking your perspective. In most surgeries, the patient is completely covered except for the small area being worked on. One reason for this is so that the surgeon empathizes *less* with you and even objectifies you to an extent. And this is a good thing. In fact, you could make the argument that you should pick a surgeon who will completely dehumanize you; your heart is just an object he's working to fix. You don't want the surgeon feeling discomfort when he's poking around inside your body cavity. You want his mind to be sharp and his focus to be on the task at hand. He's helping you because it's his job. Maybe he cares about your well-being, but he doesn't need empathy to do this. In fact, empathy could get in the way of him doing his job well.

If you take one thing away from this chapter, it should be that a good torturer could be a bit empathetic, a good surgeon may not be, and a good horror fan is probably somewhere in the middle.

This brings us to another issue with empathy: It can lead to distress and burnout. Empathy isn't a neutral feeling. If another person is in pain and you empathize with them, you feel that pain to some extent, too. It wears on you. If you're particularly high in affective empathy, you might be involuntarily catching other people's negative feelings, causing you to lose some control over your own mental state. Empathy can act as an iron-fisted dictator over your emotions. It can make it difficult *not* to feel bad. This is useful in certain, circumscribed cases. But in many instances, empathy can be detrimental to helping behavior.

Rather than building more empathy, Paul Bloom argues for what he calls rational compassion. Bloom isn't saying empathy is all bad, just that we shouldn't hold it up as an untarnished virtue. Understanding the plight of others is part of empathy, and that is clearly important. Feeling affective empathy for your offspring or close family is also important. However, empathy can sometimes make you a more effective manipulator. It can lead you to feel distress in situations where distress is unhelpful. Like nearly all traits, empathy can be good or bad depending on the context.

So when we hear statements about morbidly curious horror fans lacking empathy, we should keep two things in mind: (1) The evidence for this is not so clear, and the most recent empirical studies point to horror fans having the same ability to empathize as others, and (2) empathy isn't the pure virtue we often think it is. Compassion, or caring for others, is far more important, and horror fans are just as compassionate as anyone else.

9.

SCARY MOVIES IN SCARY TIMES

*We take refuge in make-believe terrors so the real ones
don't overwhelm us.*

—Stephen King

FINDING FACT IN FICTION

March 2020 was a terrifying time for the world. A new virus had
been spreading for a couple of months, extending its reach to every
corner of the Earth. This novel virus, dubbed COVID-19, shocked
the public and government officials alike. Public health agencies
had lost control of what the World Health Organization was now
calling a global pandemic. The United States, a country at the center of global commerce and tourism, began banning travel to and
from dozens of countries. Restaurants, bars, department stores, and
most other nonessential businesses began closing. For most people,
this experience was frightening and uncertain. It was as close to an
apocalypse as many of us have ever experienced.

The emerging pandemic was a new experience for many people,
but it reminded others of something they had seen before—something

in recent memory. Nine years before COVID-19 thrust the world into disarray, meningoencephalitis virus 1 (MEV-1) made its debut. MEV-1 resembled COVID-19 in several ways. Like COVID-19, MEV-1 was thought to have originated in bats in Asia. People infected with MEV-1 typically had a terrible cough, fatigue, headaches, and fever: all symptoms that are also commonly associated with COVID-19. Even the social response to MEV-1 eerily mirrored that of COVID-19. Travel was banned, businesses closed, essential stores were plundered for household supplies, and supposed miracle cures captured the public's imagination and became a thorn in the side of the medical community. And, as with COVID-19, a vaccine for MEV-1 was rapidly produced and distributed to the population. The MEV-1 pandemic looked like the 2020 COVID-19 pandemic in nearly every way imaginable.

Don't recall the MEV-1 outbreak? That might be because there was just one major difference between it and the COVID-19 outbreak: The MEV-1 outbreak happened in a movie.

Contagion is a 2011 movie about a global pandemic. While the movie enjoyed some success when it was released, it was far more popular in 2020 than it ever was in 2011. The disaster-themed movie went from relative obscurity to household name almost overnight. By the first week of March 2020, *Contagion* had skyrocketed to the top 10 in movie rentals at iTunes and went from being the 270th most popular film on the Warner Bros. catalog to the 2nd most popular film. Older movies sometimes have resurgences in popularity, but never anything like this.

The rise in *Contagion*'s popularity mapped astonishingly well onto the rise of COVID-19. For example, the Google Trends chart

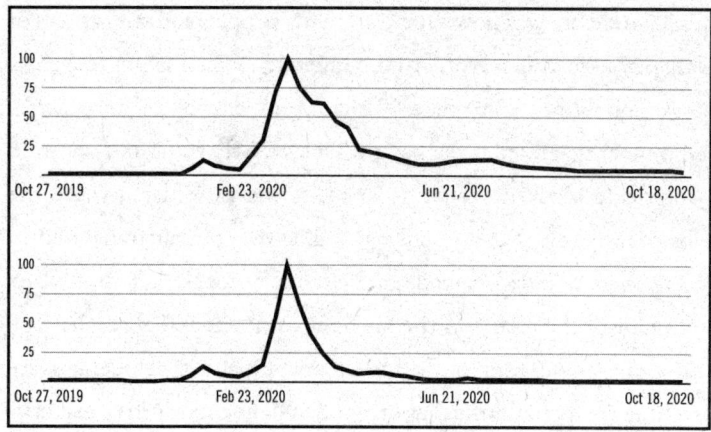

Relative interest in the Google search term "Coronavirus" (top)
and the movie *Contagion* (bottom) between November 1, 2019, and November 1,
2020. Numbers represent search interest relative to the highest point on the chart for
the term. A value of 100 is the peak popularity for the term. A value of 50 means that
the term is half as popular as it was at its peak. A score of 0 means there was not enough
data for this term. The peak popularity for both the search term "Coronavirus"
and the film *Contagion* was the week of March 15–21, 2020.

for the movie *Contagion* looks almost identical to the one for the
term "Coronavirus": There is a small bump in January followed by a
large peak in mid-March. There was also more interest in the
Google search term "pandemic movie" in March 2020 than at any
other point since data collection began in 2004.

The plot of *Contagion* wasn't conjured out of thin air. Viral outbreaks have long affected human populations. A year before *Contagion* was released, the world was coming out of the H1N1 swine flu
pandemic. This pandemic was initially very concerning to experts
because it was genetically related to one of the most dangerous outbreaks in history: the 1918 Spanish flu. The possibility of a deadly,

global pandemic was now salient to many people, and the writers of *Contagion* used this relevant and dangerous phenomenon to craft a compelling drama. The scenes of chaos caused by MEV-1 in *Contagion* were exaggerated versions of what swine flu could have been in a worst-case scenario. Luckily for us, swine flu did not cause the global disruption that it could have. The events that transpired in *Contagion* may have seemed exaggerated in 2011, but nine years later many of the scenes in the movie became shockingly realistic.

It came as no surprise to me or anyone else that people were searching for factual information about a pandemic at the most critical moment of the pandemic. There was a new threat in the world that we were unprepared for, and we needed to know what to do to keep ourselves safe. What was more surprising and much more intriguing was that many people were also looking for information about fictional pandemics at the exact same time. Why was *Contagion* surging in popularity? This caught my attention.

Intuition tells us that people will seek out escapism during stressful times like the first few months of the COVID-19 pandemic. When you have a lot going on in the real world, it can feel good to escape into a new world inside of a book, video game, or movie. But why were so many people escaping the stresses of a real pandemic by jumping into a stressful fictional world that was also plagued by a pandemic?

The halting of operations at businesses and universities in the spring of 2020 meant that most scientific research also came to a screeching halt. Closed universities meant closed laboratories, and closed laboratories meant no in-person studies. However, some of us were able to move a portion of our studies online, collecting data from participants using online versions of surveys and experiments.

My experience was a bit different from most other scientists'. The pandemic and lockdowns made some of my research difficult, but it also opened doors to research questions. I was presented with a unique opportunity to study morbid curiosity because the pandemic created a natural laboratory to observe threat perception and curiosity in just about everyone.

With all the COVID news flooding our screens and the rise in popularity of *Contagion* and other pandemic-themed movies, my first question was simple: What role is morbid curiosity playing in all of this? Although *Contagion* was skyrocketing in popularity, not everyone was a fan. Plenty of people (maybe you're one of them!) were aghast at the idea of watching a pandemic-themed movie during a real pandemic. Why terrorize my mind with a fictional pandemic *now* of all times? Give me comedies and romance, they would say. Even so, it was clear that many people were streaming pandemic movies. Who were these people, and why were they so interested in using frightening fictional worlds as an escape from a frightening real world?

I recruited people from a website called Prolific, where researchers can pay people to take part in studies or other tasks. I had the study participants rate how interested they were in watching six different genres of movies and TV shows: romance, comedy, scary/supernatural, mystery/thriller, pandemic/virus, and adventure/action. My aim was just to get at how an average person might think about genres when flipping through a streaming platform. When you went to Netflix or Hulu, what categories were you browsing?

I wanted to see whether this frightening era led people to consume more frightening media. But, as I mentioned before, not everyone was rushing to see *Contagion*. I had a hunch that the people who were doing this might be cut from a more morbidly curious cloth. To test this, I also had the participants complete the Morbid Curiosity Scale.

As I waited for my results to roll in, I started thinking back on my own experience over the past month. I had raced to watch *Contagion* myself in early March, before I conceived of the idea for the study and before I knew about the Google Trends data. At the time, I wasn't sure why I felt compelled to stream this decade-old film that I'd seen many years before. I wasn't feeling especially anxious about the pandemic, but it was filling my life with some uncertainty. Still, the feeling was closer to cautious excitement. I wasn't excited that people were getting sick, I wasn't excited that the economy might crash, and I certainly wasn't excited about being in lockdown. However, there was *something* interesting about living through this experience.

I was free from many of the costs that came with the pandemic. I didn't have kids, I wasn't worried about losing my job, and I was young and healthy. The relative risk to me was low, but the possibility to learn about a rare, potentially dangerous event was fueling my morbid curiosity. In this morbidly curious state, I had joined millions of others and turned to *Contagion*, the closest simulation of a pandemic that existed at the time.

I clenched my jaw in anticipation as the results of my study poured in. A wave of relief washed over me as I began to analyze the data. My morbidly curious participants reported that they were much more interested in watching pandemic movies in the upcoming week than they usually were. This was especially interesting since this data was collected in April 2020, just as the US was entering an uncertain phase of the pandemic. Morbidly curious people were seeking out fictional simulations of this new viral threat.

Of course, this data might have been less interesting if morbidly curious people were just watching more movies of all kinds. After all, people were quarantining in their homes with not much else to do besides doomscroll social media and binge-watch Netflix. However, I found no correlation between morbid curiosity and increased interest in other genres like comedy, romance, or action movies. Morbidly curious people were no more or less interested in those kinds of movies. However, there was one genre that morbidly curious people were streaming in droves.

SEEKING OUT SCARES

I was seeing something even more interesting than the resurgence of *Contagion* emerging from my data. While morbidly curious people were indeed more interested in pandemic movies, they also expressed greater interest in scary movies more broadly. Google Trends data on searches for "horror" (film genre) and "scary movies" (search term) corroborated this finding as well. Searches for these terms peaked in October 2020 in anticipation of Halloween, as they do every year, but 2020's Halloween season saw the most interest in those terms since data collection began in 2004.

The 2020 box office numbers also back up this finding. In any given year, horror receives around 6 percent of the market share of tickets, putting the genre in sixth place behind thriller/suspense (which arguably includes many horror films, but I'll leave that discussion for another time), comedy, drama, action, and adventure. Horror's market share waxed and waned between 1995 and 2021. But, aside from a very successful year in 2017 due to the release of three blockbuster films (*Split*, *Get Out*, and *It*), horror's market share never strayed too far from 6 percent.

This changed in 2020 when the horror genre nearly doubled its average annual box office market share. In fact, horror captured the largest share of the box office in its history during the first year of the pandemic. This didn't seem to be a fluke, either: Horror went on to nab an even larger share of the box office in the second year of the pandemic. Fictional scares were booming during one of the scariest moments in recent history.

SCARE RX

In early April 2020 an editor at *New Scientist* named Penny Sarchet posed an interesting question on social media. She asked if people who watch more apocalyptic and horror movies would be more resilient to the trauma of the COVID-19 pandemic. I think Penny may have asked this a bit tongue in cheek, but when I saw her question, I immediately messaged my frequent collaborator, Mathias Clasen. What a great idea for a study!

The notion that horror fans might be more resilient during a pandemic is based on the idea that horror stories can act as a form of play or, more specifically, scary play. Sometimes scary play is physical, like what we see with haunted attractions. However, it takes on a more cognitive form with fictional stories, where we can play with certain interactions or situations without actually experiencing them.

For quite some time, my colleagues and I had been theorizing that fictional scary play, such as watching horror movies or reading horror novels, could serve as preparation for scary events. I don't mean that it's a *literal* preparation. When we watch *Halloween* or *Friday the 13th*, the most important information isn't learning how to escape a masked man with a large, bladed weapon. Instead, the key learning component is often a form of emotional practice. We can practice how to regulate and cope with fear, anxiety, and other feelings that would arise in dangerous or otherwise frightening situations. When we engage with the horror genre, we are playing with fear.

PANDEMIC PRACTICE

Fear and anxiety are things that most people try to avoid in their daily life, and for good reason. However, anxiety-inducing or fearful things are bound to happen to us at some point or another, and it benefits us to be prepared in those situations.

That being said, experiencing a fictional situation that resembles a real-world scenario could also literally prepare you for that situation. Simulated methods of practice are common in many industries. A flight simulator is a great example of fictional training; you take away all the danger associated with a risky situation and keep as much of the learning benefits as possible. During a pandemic, an accurately portrayed fictional scenario of a pandemic could provide some practical knowledge about what pandemics are like in addition to the emotional practice of dealing with fear and anxiety.

With this in mind, Mathias and I wanted to answer three main questions with our study: (1) Do people who are fans of horror movies report greater psychological resilience during the COVID-19 pandemic? (2) Do morbidly curious people report greater psychological resilience during the COVID-19 pandemic? And, (3) Did people who had seen more "prepper movies" (movies with end-of-the-world themes) feel more prepared for the COVID-19 pandemic? In other words, our study aimed to answer whether morbid curiosity could actually provide some benefits when danger strikes.

Our first task was to figure out how to measure resilience. While many of the existing questionnaires did a great job of assessing resilience to one-time events like natural disasters, terrorist attacks, and muggings, they weren't as useful for measuring resilience to events that are drawn out, like a pandemic. We pulled as many sensible questions as we could from previously validated scales, modified the wording if needed, and combined them with a few new questions to form what we called the Pandemic Psychological Resilience Scale.

The scale consists of twelve items that measure two types of resilience. The first type of resilience is called positive resilience. Positive resilience refers to your ability to experience positive emotional states and meaning during difficult times. The second kind of resilience is resilience to psychological distress. This refers to dampened physiological or behavioral symptoms of stress during a difficult time. Someone with strong positive resilience during the pandemic would believe in their ability to get through it and feel positive about the future. Someone with strong resilience to psychological distress might be more resistant to insomnia and symptoms of anxiety during the pandemic. *Higher* scores on the positive resilience (PR) questions and *lower* scores on the psychological distress (PD) questions indicate better psychological resilience. Participants who took the survey were asked to report their answers on a 7-point scale from strongly disagree to strongly agree.

1. During the pandemic, I have been more depressed than usual. (PD)

2. Compared to how I usually feel, I have been more nervous and anxious during the pandemic. (PD)

3. I am more irritable than usual. (PD)

4. I haven't been sleeping well since the pandemic started. (PD)

5. I have been taking the news about the pandemic in stride. (PR)

6. I have been able to find things to enjoy during the pandemic. (PR)

7. I feel positive about the future. (PR)

8. I have found some aspects of the pandemic to be interesting. (PR)

9. I believe in my ability to get through these difficult times. (PR)

10. I know that I can get through these uncertain times. (PR)

11. Life has felt meaningful during the pandemic. (PR)

12. Despite troubles, I have been able to find things to laugh about. (PR)

There are many reasons why someone might be more resilient during a pandemic. Some of these reasons might be based on personality. Perhaps they are more introverted or less neurotic than the average person, so lockdowns and a scary new virus may not be as disruptive to their daily life. Other reasons for resilience might be situational. Maybe they make a lot of money or are young and healthy and are less at risk.

With this in mind, my colleagues and I made sure to control for factors like these that might influence resilience in our analyses. We asked people about their age, sex, and income. We also had them take a personality test so that we could account for general personality in our analyses. In this case, we controlled for the Big Five personality traits: openness to experience, agreeableness, extraversion, conscientiousness, and neuroticism. These five traits have been shown to influence a wide variety of life outcomes and likely played some role in psychological resilience during the pandemic. Finally, we controlled for how much people like to watch movies and TV shows in general. After all, people who are good at engaging in escapism through movies and TV shows might simply be better at dealing with (or at least momentarily escaping from) difficult life circumstances.

As we predicted, horror fans and morbidly curious people in our study were experiencing higher levels of resilience during the pandemic, even when statistically controlling for other personality traits and life circumstances. We also found that people who liked prepper movies were more likely to feel prepared for the pandemic. Morbid curiosity seemed to be providing a buffer to the anxiety-inducing pandemic. There were some interesting nuances, though.

While the strongest predictor of being a horror fan is being morbidly curious, there isn't a perfect one-to-one correlation. Enjoying horror entertainment is simply a common expression of morbid curiosity, and some people who are morbidly curious may not enjoy the horror genre as much as others. In our data, there were some slight differences in the kind of resilience that people experienced depending on whether we looked at morbid curiosity or horror fandom. When we isolated the morbid curiosity variable, we found that morbidly curious people scored much higher in positive resilience; they found ways to enjoy life during the pandemic, had a positive outlook, found meaning in life, and even found some aspects of the pandemic to be interesting. When looking at horror fans specifically, however, we found that they were much more resilient to psychological distress during the pandemic; they weren't experiencing the same negative shift in anxiety, sleeplessness, or irritability that non–horror fans were experiencing. When you've experienced fictional nightmares dozens of times, a real nightmare is a little less jarring.

Now, you might be thinking, "Maybe people who like horror movies are just more resilient to distressing experiences by nature—hence why they like horror movies!" Perhaps you're right. Intuition certainly would suggest this. Surely only people who easily endure distress, or even enjoy it, would be horror fans, right?

One reason this interpretation may not be accurate is that we controlled for neuroticism in our analyses. People high in neuroticism don't tend to endure distress very well and are often more anxious. However, even when statistically accounting for levels of neuroticism, we found that horror fans and morbidly curious people were more resilient.

Another reason that interpretation may not be accurate is that some research suggests that horror fans and morbidly curious people tend to, on average, be a little *more* anxious by nature.

SCAREDY-CATS LOVE SCARY STORIES

Give people any number of anxiety assessments and ask them if they like horror movies, and you'll find a small but consistent association between high anxiety and horror fandom. Contrary to what some might believe, horror fans aren't just a bunch of hard-hearted adrenaline junkies. In some cases, they're more anxious than those who dislike horror. This extends to horror filmmakers and writers, too. Mike Flanagan, creator of terrifying flicks such as *Hush* and *The Haunting of Hill House*, has stated that he couldn't watch horror movies or read horror novels as a kid because they scared him too much.

Back in the early 2000s, before movie rental stores went extinct, media researchers Yuliya Strizhakova and Marina Krcmar conducted a study to see how a person's mood affected the movies they rented. To test this, they set up shop in front of a movie rental store from 3:00 p.m. until closing time every night for a week. As customers came in to rent movies, they were asked about their current mood: how happy, sad, afraid, nervous, angry, energetic, calm, bored, and unpleasant were they feeling? When the customers exited the store, the researchers took note of which movies they rented and what genre they were.

Strizhakova and Krcmar expected people who were feeling nervous to rent more soothing and easygoing movies, like comedies. This makes intuitive sense and even aligned with a popular media psychology theory that said that if you are overaroused, you'll pick a form of entertainment or escapism that is pleasant and soothing. This theory would predict that people try to manage their mood by selecting entertainment that is the opposite of how they are feeling. Makes enough sense, right?

You can imagine how surprised the researchers were when they found that nervous people were actually *more* likely to rent horror movies than any other genre. It's possible, you might say, that people were feeling nervous *because* they were about to rent a horror movie. Maybe that's true. Of course, this would mean most participants knew exactly what they wanted to rent before going in. This was probably not the case—after all, how often do you open Netflix already knowing exactly what you want to watch? And even if it was, feeling anxious about a movie you haven't even rented yet would suggest that horror movie fans are a *really* anxious bunch.

An alternative hypothesis is that people who are more likely to feel nervous are also more likely to enjoy horror. It sounds a bit counterintuitive at first, but this hypothesis fits with what I and others have been finding in our research.

A group of researchers from the University of Pennsylvania and Cambridge University looked into how someone's personality might predict how much they liked certain genres of movies. To do this, they used data from a Facebook app called myPersonality that ran from 2007 to 2012. MyPersonality allowed Facebook users to take scientific surveys and discover how they scored on various measures of personality. One of the more popular measures was a Big Five index of personality that told people how they scored on conscientiousness, openness to experience, extraversion, agreeableness, and neuroticism.

Because the results were connected to users' Facebook accounts, the researchers were able to cross-reference the users' personality scores with movie pages they had liked on Facebook. The movies were then cross-referenced with information from IMDb.com, including genre and plot keywords. The resulting dataset was massive: over eight hundred films and 3.5 million Big Five surveys from over forty countries.

The paper is full of incredibly interesting findings. But one of the most interesting bits is the fact that, on average, people who liked movies categorized as horror scored higher in neuroticism, a trait characterized by high anxiety. As strange as it sounds, being a more anxious person predicted liking anxiety-inducing movies.

Digging deeper into the data, the researchers pulled keywords from the plots of each movie and categorized them into themes such as death, religion, money, home, leisure, and work. These keywords and themes were then tested against the users' Big Five personality results. Consistent with their first study, the researchers found that more anxious people tended to like movies with themes of death and anxiety. Movies with plot keywords like "serial killer," "ghost," and "disfigurement" were also more likely to be liked by the anxious participants.

Serial killer, ghost, and disfigurement. Those align quite well with the four categories on my Morbid Curiosity Scale: minds of dangerous people, violence, the paranormal, and bodily injuries. As I would soon come to realize, morbid curiosity and anxiety share some important features. These shared, core features help explain the peculiar paradox of anxious people seeking out and enjoying movies that aim to make their audiences feel anxious and afraid. But the power of scary movies goes beyond mere entertainment. These films may also provide some therapeutic benefits.

10.

TERRIFYING THERAPY

But I found that if I could will myself to make it through
a scary scene without covering my eyes, I was getting
braver in controlled increments. That exercise afforded
me something I could carry into my life.

—*Mike Flanagan*

LOOKING FOR DANGER

One of the most powerful attentional biases in human psychology is
the threat bias. Humans are drawn to any hint of a potential threat,
and this attentional bias is amplified in people with anxiety. Though it
is sometimes used synonymously with fear, anxiety differs in an important way. Fear is an emotion that evolved because it aided in avoiding a clear and present threat: A man with an ax is chasing after me.
Anxiety evolved because it helped protect our species from uncertain
or future threats: *What if* a man with an ax were chasing me? What
tactics would he use? What tactics would I use? Would I survive?

We are all familiar with the signs of anxiety: your heart races,
you begin breathing rapidly, and your mind darts between different

actions you could take, weighing the potential outcomes. Anxiety gets a bad rap, but a certain level of anxiety is adaptive and necessary to respond adequately to the challenges of life; it's a motivator of behavior. Without *any* anxiety, we would hardly have the motivation to get out of bed in the morning. Of course, this is not the type of anxiety that we tend to think of when we hear the word. Rather, we tend to think of anxiety in its excessive form, when it makes us uncomfortable and interferes with our daily life.

Anxiety increases vigilance, which focuses attention to a potential threat and intensifies immersion. This immersion factor is what makes an anxiety attack so difficult to shake. It's easy to get caught in cycles of rumination because anxiety motivates you to think about threatening situations, which makes the threat feel more present, which further amplifies your vigilance, which increases attention to threatening situations . . . and so on and so forth.

Some studies using virtual reality have shown that both anxiety in the moment and anxiety as a stable personality trait can influence immersion. For example, people report feeling much more immersed in a virtual reality game when the environment is anxiety inducing. Similarly, individuals with a clinically diagnosed anxiety disorder report feeling more present during virtual reality exposure therapy than those without an anxiety diagnosis.

The increased vigilance motivation to learn about threats that occurs when you are anxious can act as fuel for your morbid curiosity. This is sometimes a bad thing. If you can't identify a threat, then your vigilance mechanisms turn up even more, leading to those terrible cycles of anxious rumination. However, morbid curiosity can also be used to overcome your anxiety. This might sound a bit abstract, so let's use watching a horror movie as an example to see how morbid curiosity can be harnessed to help someone when they are feeling anxious.

HORROR TO THE RESCUE

Horror movies can provide a way for you to hack and redirect your vigilance system. They act as a lure for an anxious mind, using a threat-centric plot to capture and hold the viewer's attention. If you're feeling anxious and having trouble kicking the cycle of rumination, the threat-focused plot of a horror movie might be able to interrupt the cycle by providing a new, salient threat for your mind to latch on to. When information about a threat is presented through a visually compelling horror story, that information can outcompete the other sources of your anxiety.

Once it has your attention, a horror film serves as a dark playground in which your mind's worries can run amok. There can be stigma associated with expressing anxiety in the real world, but the stigma is reversed in a horror movie, where you are *expected* to feel anxious and afraid. If you don't feel some anxiety or fear, then the horror movie has arguably not succeeded in its goal. Instead of suppressing your anxious feelings, you can express them freely.

Expressing emotions can be particularly important for learning effective emotion regulation. Suppression is a common tactic people employ when they're feeling anxious. While it is a useful tool in some instances, it's not great for learning to overcome anxiety. Suppression can sometimes result in rebounds of anxiety and difficulty in everyday social situations because your inner feelings do not match your outward expression. You walk around with your mask of tranquility, but inside your mind is a maze of worries. Horror allows you to take off your mask. It's a safe space for you to express your anxiety, allowing you to come to terms with it and learn to manage it more effectively than you could if you suppressed it.

At this point, you're partway through the horror movie and your mind is still on high alert, but the source of your anxiety has shifted. Now you're feeling anxious about the killer or monster in the movie instead of whatever it was you were feeling anxious about before. Once this happens, you're handed the reins, and you gain a sense of control over the source of the anxiety. This sense of control is critical to horror being a good conduit for regulating anxiety. When feeling anxious, people often have little perceived control over their anxiety. When we increase our perceived control over a stressor, we reduce activation in areas of the brain that respond to threat-related uncertainty. When you're in control, a threat becomes less threatening.

If you're feeling anxious while watching a horror film, you have several avenues of potential control or regulation over the source of the anxiety. For example, if you are feeling too anxious you can watch the movie with the lights on or volume turned down. These tactics serve to decrease immersion, which, while necessary to initially draw you in, may need to be reduced during certain parts of the movie for you to achieve an optimal experience.

You also have some control over the threat itself. Once the monster makes an appearance on-screen, simple behaviors like covering your eyes can reduce fear and lead to a feeling of control over the situation. A horror movie creates anxiety that is controllable by the viewer in a way that is difficult or impossible to achieve outside of a fictional world. The level of experienced anxiety becomes an adjustable choice the viewer makes when watching a horror movie.

Unlike anxiety stemming from threats in the real world, horror-fiction-induced anxiety is rooted in a clear source. It's more easily managed and it has a clear end point. These factors are key in taking the anxiety that you are feeling and slowly turning it down. Being able to identify a clear source of anxiety (i.e., the villain or monster in the movie) allows you to act against it. You have strategies that you can use to control how intense it feels (e.g., turning down the volume, turning on the lights, or pausing the movie). This allows you to adjust the anxiety to a manageable level and regulate your feelings. And, after about ninety minutes, the movie-related anxiety will fade as the credits begin to roll.

EXITING THE CYCLE

We've just seen how a horror movie can help with anxiety at the psychological level. However, there is a biological aspect to this as well. When we go through a stressful experience, our body goes through changes that prepare us for fight or flight.

The part of our nervous system that connects to our vital organs to enact changes during times of threat is called the autonomic nervous system. It controls things like heart rate, blood pressure, digestion, pupil dilation, and the release of hormones that mediate these physiological processes. The autonomic nervous system has two branches that control different aspects of our physiology: the sympathetic nervous system and the parasympathetic nervous system.

Both these systems are always active to some degree, but stressful or threatening situations cause the sympathetic nervous system to ramp up. Increased sympathetic nervous system activity leads to a rush of adrenaline, increased heart rate, dilated pupils, and increased blood flow to organs and muscles—all those sensations you feel when you're scared for your life. When the threatening situation is eliminated, the sympathetic nervous system activity decreases and parasympathetic nervous system activity ramps up. The parasympathetic nervous system helps reverse some of the sympathetic nervous system activity; it slows heart rate, increases digestion and salivation, and allows the pupils to constrict. An easy way to remember the difference between these two systems is that the sympathetic nervous system promotes "fight or flight" while the parasympathetic nervous system aids in "rest and digest."

If you've ever gone through an exciting and intense experience like a haunted attraction during Halloween, you've experienced this process. The buildup of excitement and anxiety as you wait in line to enter the haunt is your sympathetic nervous system ramping up and preparing you to flee the monsters inside the haunted house. Your heart may still be racing as you exit the haunt, but then you breathe a sigh of relief. You begin to feel slightly elated—that's the sympathetic nervous system slowing down and the parasympathetic nervous system kicking into gear. Scary play, like what occurs when we watch horror movies or run through haunted houses, allows our bodies to complete this cycle and achieve the rest-and-relaxation component without getting stuck in the anxious cycle of high sympathetic nervous system activity with nowhere to go.

Margee Kerr is an expert on the science of fear and one of the few researchers who has used haunted attractions as a way to study scary play. In one study, she teamed up with neuroscientist Greg Siegle to see how scary play impacts brain reactivity and relaxation. The researchers set up shop in a small room at a haunted attraction called ScareHouse in Pittsburgh, Pennsylvania. Inside the room, visitors filled out questionnaires about their mood and completed simple tasks while their brain activity was recorded EEG.

After their EEG session, the participants braved their way through the haunted house, running through rooms filled with evil clowns and chain-saw-wielding killers. When they returned to the testing room for a follow-up EEG session, Kerr and her team found that participants had lower levels of anxiety than they did before entering the haunt. They also found that the participants' brains were less reactive across a variety of tasks following the scary play experience. In other words, surviving the onslaught of scare actors in a haunted house appeared to produce a calming, almost peaceful feeling that persisted even when the participants were presented with unsettling images or asked to ruminate on a personal negative experience.

Horror entertainment and other forms of scary play can serve as more than a simple distraction when it comes to anxiety. A good, scary horror film has the power to reach into a vicious cycle of rumination and grab our mind's attention. Once it has hold of our attention, a horror movie can then monopolize the anxious feelings, pushing out daily worries. Once your anxiety targets the movie rather

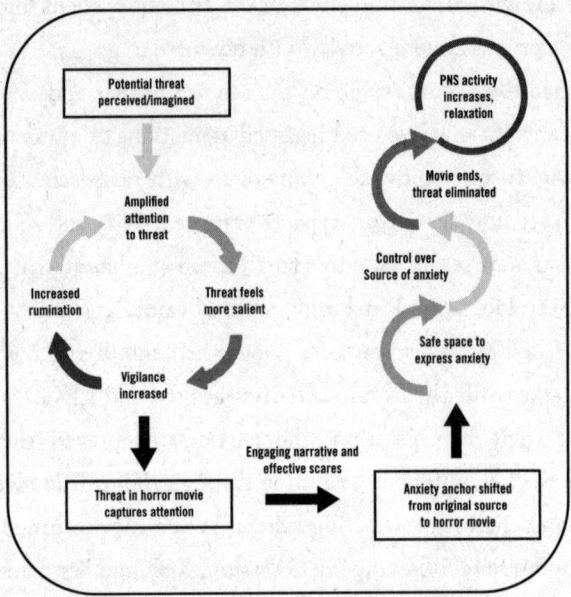

The process by which a horror movie could disengage the viewer
from a cycle of rumination and ease anxiety symptoms.

than whatever you were initially ruminating about, you are set on a path that is more conducive to calming the anxious feelings.

A horror movie is a safe place for you to express your anxiety, eliminating the feeling that you need to suppress your negative emotions. It also allows you to control the intensity of the anxiety; you could watch with the lights on, turn the sound down, or cover your eyes during the scariest parts. Importantly, the new, fictional source of your anxiety has a short lifespan. After about ninety minutes, the threat disappears, tricking your mind into thinking you have escaped or overcome the threat. This allows the parasympathetic nervous system to kick into gear and decrease the symptoms associated with anxiety.

As with most treatments, this process may not work for everyone. The science behind how horror can help with anxiety is still being uncovered. However, the preliminary investigations are producing promising results. As we'll see in the next chapter, there are some encouraging clinical trials that have shown how scary games can help children overcome anxiety by teaching them emotion regulation skills.

BUILDING LONG-TERM RESILIENCE

While the potential for short-term relief from anxiety is intriguing, the real question is whether repeated exposure to these experiences could create long-term change. Can a lifetime of being morbidly curious somehow benefit your mental well-being? Could horror movies strengthen your resilience? Can scary play serve as terrifying therapy?

Scary play may help people overcome anxiety and build resilience by relying on the same principles as exposure therapy, one of the most empirically validated treatments for anxiety. Exposure therapy has been proven to be effective for a wide range of anxiety diagnoses, including specific phobias, OCD, PTSD, social phobia, panic disorder, and generalized anxiety disorder.

Exposure therapy decreases the unmanageable amount of anxiety that results from exposure to a stimulus through habituation and fear extinction. As the anxious person is exposed more and more to what they fear, the extreme physiological reactions tend to decrease. Exposure therapy also allows someone to break patterns of avoidance. Avoiding something that causes anxiety is a common coping mechanism that offers short-term relief but isn't very effective for dealing with chronic anxiety. One way to break the pattern of avoidance is to prove to yourself that being exposed to an anxiety-inducing stimulus doesn't result in the extremely negative consequences that you fear it will. Once this happens, you can create new associations with the feared stimulus. For example, you might learn over time that the intense sensations you feel can be interpreted as excitement rather than anxiety. When all of this works together, you can gain a sense of self-efficacy; you become more confident in your ability to deal with and overcome feelings of dread, fear, or anxiety.

Let's go back to our horror movie example for a moment. When you sit down to watch a horror movie, you are probably not exposing yourself to a particular phobia (though I suppose some arachnophobes could watch *Eight Legged Freaks* or ophidiophobes could watch *Anaconda*). But you *are* exposing yourself to feelings of fear and anxiety and you *are* exposing yourself to the physiological symptoms that make anxiety feel uncomfortable. This type of exposure is called interoceptive exposure.

The great thing about interoceptive exposure is that the benefits can show up across a wide variety of situations. You might not conquer a phobia of spiders by watching a ghost movie, but you do experience habituation to the somatic sensations associated with anxiety, and you do experience feelings of self-efficacy when you make it through a session. These can help you when you are faced with your phobia. You can learn that the extreme sensations that accompany anxiety may not correlate strongly with the actual consequences that you will experience. Anxiety makes a bad thing seem a lot worse than it is. Interoceptive exposure helps show you that your exaggerated feelings of dread aren't always good indicators of how bad something really is.

It's not just passively experiencing anxiety in a safe context that is beneficial. While that might contribute to habituation, it wouldn't necessarily help build long-term skills for handling anxiety. Instead, skills for resilience might be built by taking an active approach to regulating how anxious you feel. When you're watching a scary movie and you get to a scene that is too intense, you can pause the movie and practice calming yourself down—something that is much more difficult to achieve outside the safety of your couch and the fictional world of the movie. By experiencing anxiety in a safe situation where you will not bear any real consequences, you are freer to explore your own emotions and gain a better understanding of how to navigate anxious thoughts and feelings.

Horror films and haunted houses often tout how scary they are to drum up excitement. The assumption behind this marketing tactic is that customers always want more fear when it comes to horror. However, evidence from my lab suggests that many horror fans take an active approach to regulating their fear—both up and down—when watching scary movies or engaging in other kinds of scary play. Presumably, they do this to regulate their arousal levels for an optimal level of scariness. Like a dreadful Goldilocks, many horror fans want their monsters not too scary, and not too harmless, but just right in terms of terror.

THE SWEET SPOT OF FEAR

Scary play can be a tricky thing to study in the lab. For understandable reasons, ethics committees and institutional review boards furrow their brows at studies that propose to terrify participants for money. Still, gaining approval for a study on scary play isn't even the biggest hurdle. It's fairly difficult to induce genuine fear and anxiety in participants in a laboratory setting, especially when you're creating a playful situation. Many studies use short scenes from horror movies as a way to induce acute fear and anxiety. While this method has its merits, an out-of-context scene from a horror movie isn't the best representation of scary play.

Some of the most interesting work on the psychological effects and possible benefits of scary play comes from Danish horror scholar Mathias Clasen. He and his team set up a field site at a haunted house attraction to study how people regulated their fear and anxiety during the experience. The researchers found that visitors used a combination of strategies to regulate their fear levels throughout the experience. When the visitors wanted to feel more afraid, they took actions to immerse themselves in the experience: They focused more on the scares, they imagined that the scenario could be real, they engaged in the story that accompanied the experience, and they let themselves scream in terror. Sometimes the scares were too intense, and visitors used strategies to decrease immersion by reminding themselves that the scary parts were not real, trying to find humor in the situation, looking away from the scare actors, and holding on to friends for comfort. The haunt-goers were active participants in the experience; they engaged in tactics that helped them manipulate how afraid they felt.

I'd read this study as a young graduate student and I was excited about the idea of testing fear in a setting like a haunted house. At the time, no other researchers were really conducting research at haunted houses, so I reached out to Mathias to learn more. As it so happened, we were both planning on being at the same academic conference several weeks later. We met up at the conference and got along really well, so he invited me to Denmark to work with him on a follow-up study. For me, this was a dream start to my career. I was getting in on the groundwork of some of the most exciting scientific work on fear and scary play.

I left for Denmark that October to take part in my first haunted house field study. I spent my first week in Denmark planning some of the logistics of the study with Mathias and his two colleagues, Marc Andersen and Uffe Schjoedt. Since their previous study found that participants were using strategies to regulate their fear in the haunt, we wondered if there might be a sweet spot of fear that people would aim for. To investigate this, we decided to measure the visitors' heart rates throughout the haunt and interview them after they came running out. We also decided to set up video cameras throughout the haunt to capture people's reactions to different scares. If people really were trying to regulate how afraid they were, we reasoned that this might be reflected in their heart rates, behavioral expressions, and reported levels of fear and enjoyment.

On Friday morning, we packed a car full of cables, computers, video cameras, and chest straps that measure heart rate. We drove about an hour and a half to a place called Vejle, a charming little Danish town nestled in a swatch of small hills. We turned down an unmarked road with trees on both sides. The road was long and winding, and the trees blocked out most of what little diffused light the cloudy sky offered. We were driving into the bowels of a dark forest, and it felt as if the haunt had begun before we'd even arrived. We finally came to a clearing and an old concrete and steel building emerged. It was an abandoned fishery. Well, mostly abandoned: The building now served as the headquarters for the haunted house company Dystopia Entertainment.

As soon as we arrived, we met with Jonas, the "Architect of Fear" and owner of Dystopia, to discuss the logistics of the study. We then spent the rest of the morning and afternoon setting up our research station. We staged an area near the entrance where we could number participants, affix the heart rate monitors, and set up a centralized location for our computers. We then searched for rooms that had some of the best jump scares to hide our video cameras.

We finished our setup just moments before the first haunt visitors arrived. As people entered Dystopia, they would first visit our research station, where they would be given a large sticker with their participant number, much like the kind runners wear during a marathon. They would then answer a few questions about themselves: their age, sex, expectations about the haunt, and whether they had been to Dystopia or any other haunted house before. Each member of the group would then slip on a chest strap that monitored their heart rate before being ushered into the haunt.

After the groups emerged from their experience, sweaty and their hearts beating out of their chests, they filled out a second questionnaire. This one asked the participants to recall what they had just experienced—how scared were they during the experience? How much fun did they have? Did they feel as if the experience was a type of play? Finally, they slipped off the heart rate monitors and we uploaded their data to our computer. We ran through this procedure the rest of the night and the following night, gathering as much data as possible. After a long weekend of scares and data collection, we packed up our equipment and headed back to the lab to analyze the results.

Our data from the haunt suggested that more fear isn't always better; enjoyment did not continuously increase with more fear. Instead, we found more of a curvilinear relationship. As ratings of fear increased, ratings of enjoyment increased to a point before they began to decline again. The shape of this relationship is something like an inverted U, where there is a peak amount of enjoyment at a moderate amount of fear. In this case, a reported fear of about a 6 or 7 out of 10 corresponded with the highest degree of fun.

The heart rate data told a similar story. For our heart rate data, we looked at something called heart rate variability, or HRV. This measures the variation in the time between heartbeats, which is a good way to capture subtle changes that result from the push and pull of different aspects of the autonomic nervous system. Because it can measure subtle changes better than simple heartbeats per minute, HRV is good for capturing moment-to-moment stressors, like a chain-saw-wielding pig-man chasing you down a dark hallway of an abandoned fishery.

We found that a moderate degree of HRV corresponded with the most enjoyment, while too much or too little HRV was associated with less enjoyment. In other words, physiological arousal also showed an inverted-U-shape relationship with enjoyment. Taken together with the self-report data, this study suggests that people really do have a sweet spot, both physiologically and subjectively, when it comes to fear. Too scary, and it stops being fun; not scary enough, and it's not exciting. The best horror doesn't push us past our limits. It pushes us just to the edge of them.

Not everyone has the same sweet spot when it comes to fear. Some people want the chain-saw-wielding maniac in the haunt to chase them. Others need only a little stimulation. A scary book or podcast gets them to their Goldilocks zone. Horror fans fall all along this spectrum. Someone who thrives on extreme haunted houses is not "more" of a horror fan or more morbidly curious than someone who has never been to a haunt but reads every horror novel they can get their hands on. It's not about how scared you get or how much of a scare you can handle. It's about seeking out and enjoying playful situations that scare you.

Those with a higher sweet spot of fear seek out more extreme versions of horror. People with a lower threshold will seek out horror that is more controllable: a movie they can pause or a book they can put down. The more effort that is required to become immersed, the more control you have over your fear regulation. For those with lower sweet spots of fear, more control usually leads to a better experience.

Although fear is central to horror, it's not the feeling of fear per se that is always sought after. So what is it, then, that people get out of horror?

THREE TYPES OF HORROR FANS

It's an age-old question: Why do some people enjoy frightful experiences? What is it about the horror genre that draws an audience?

As we know, opportunities to learn threat-related information with little to no cost to us are powerfully attractive, and we often seek them out. These opportunities are exactly what the horror genre offers. Horror dexterously tugs at the ancient strings of the threat-detection and predator-avoidance systems in the brain. It's candy for our anxious minds. And much like how the sweetness of candy signals to our mind that it is an inexpensive source of valuable calories, the experience of fear in a place of relative safety signals an inexpensive source of valuable information.

There's a common (mis)perception that the only appeal of horror entertainment is the rush you get when you are scared. The creeping suspense, the spooky atmosphere, and the sudden appearance of the monster in a movie certainly do give those watching a boost of adrenaline. And, for some horror fans, this is what they seek. The tingling anxiety and jolts of fear are perceived as pleasurable for some people. For them, the experience of a horror movie is much like the experience sought after from roller coasters or skydiving. It's the rush they're after. My colleagues and I at the Recreational Fear Lab call this type of horror fan the Adrenaline Junkie.

Several psychological studies were conducted in the 1980s showing that people who were high in a personality trait called sensation-seeking reported more enjoyment of horror movies. These people will often seek out varied, complex, and novel experiences in their lives. It's the intense feelings associated with these kinds of experiences that sensation seekers enjoy. Even experiences that might be risky or dangerous or elicit feelings of fear (and sometimes especially those kinds of experiences) are subjectively interpreted as exciting and enjoyable.

Watching a scary movie or fighting your way through a haunted house is a reliable way to experience extreme sensations. Because of this, the horror genre does tend to be a honeypot for people who score high in sensation-seeking. Sensation seekers often seek out higher-intensity experiences as well, such as extreme sports or thrilling theme park rides.

A large part of my research program involves identifying common beliefs about horror fans and conducting research to see if there is any truth to these stereotypes. One of these stereotypes is that horror fans only really like horror for the adrenaline rush they get. After all, how else could seemingly normal people enjoy such macabre entertainment? Despite this clearly being true for some horror fans, I was skeptical that it held true for *all*, or even most, horror fans. After all, there are plenty of ways to get an adrenaline rush, so why horror entertainment?

Haunts often compete with one another to offer the most extreme experiences. To an even greater extent than horror movies, haunts market themselves as terrifying, daring potential customers to brave the experience. Haunts trade in high-sensation experiences. Of all the different types of horror entertainment where one might find Adrenaline Junkies, they should be most concentrated at haunts. If my hypothesis that not all horror fans are Adrenaline Junkies was going to be wrong in any particular context, it would be wrong at a haunt. So that's where I decided to test it.

First, I needed a way to actually measure whether someone was an Adrenaline Junkie, and if they weren't, to understand why were they seeking out horror. One way to do this would be to simply give them a sensation-seeking scale. However, this would only really tell me whether someone generally was or was not an Adrenaline Junkie.

If people were seeking out horror for other reasons, I wouldn't really know what those were. So I set out to make my own horror fan typology that could identify the different types of horror fans.

I took dozens of statements from horror blogs, magazines, news articles, and comment threads for responses that centered around the statement "why I like horror movies" and presented them to several hundred horror fans. I then used a statistical technique that identifies clusters of answers, similar to how personality tests are created. I found that three clusters, or "factors," best explained the data I had. One of these factors included participant agreement with statements like "I love the adrenaline rush I get from watching horror movies" and "I go to horror movies because I love the feeling of being scared." As you might have guessed, my colleagues and I identified this factor as the Adrenaline Junkie.

Another factor that emerged included participant agreement with statements like "I have nightmares after watching horror movies" and "Even though I know horror movies are not real, I still get really scared while watching them." These statements reflected a genuine fear of horror movies. People who scored high in this area didn't necessarily enjoy horror for the extreme sensations that come from feeling scared. They often felt afraid long after the movie ended. Yet, they still reported enjoying horror movies. We decided to call this group the White Knucklers—the name coming from the white color you get on your knuckles when you clench your fist in fear.

We anticipated that we might find Adrenaline Junkies and White Knucklers as independent factors in our study. A few previous studies had hinted at the existence of these groups, including a study by my colleagues at the Recreational Fear Lab. However, a third factor emerged that was new and somewhat unexpected. It included participant agreement with statements like "Watching horror movies helps me control feelings of anxiety or depression" and "Watching horror movies is a way for me to cope with the real world." This factor centered around a theme of using horror to explore existential thoughts and understand negative emotions. People in this group appeared to use the darker side of life to cope with difficulties they experienced. So we decided to call this group the Dark Copers.

With our new scale, my research team and I once again found ourselves spending the weekend at Dystopia Haunted House in Vejle, Denmark. This time, we set up a large tent outside of the haunt, which we decorated with skeletons, fake blood, and spooky

Our research station outside of Dystopia Haunted House.

music. We set up tables with tablets and QR codes where participants could take surveys both before they entered the haunt and after they exited. Just as the visitors began arriving, we put on our
Horror Research Team lab coats, splashed them with fake blood,
and got to work.

Our three horror-fan types replicated beautifully with the Danish participants at Dystopia. We found people across the horror
spectrum at the haunt, not just Adrenaline Junkies. We also looked
into what potential benefits these different groups got from their
experience at the haunted house. When people finished the haunt
and reflected on their experience, what did they think was useful or
good about it? Here's where things really got interesting.

As you might expect, the Adrenaline Junkies reported feeling
great after the haunt. For them, the benefits of the haunt mostly
came down to an immediate mood boost from the exciting experience, much like one gets from skydiving or bungee jumping. The
White Knucklers told us they felt fine, but they weren't on an adrenaline high like the Adrenaline Junkies. In general, there was no relationship between scoring high in the White Knuckler category
and feeling especially good after the haunt. Rather than a mood
boost from the high-sensation experience, the White Knucklers got
something a little more intellectual and personal. They reported
that they had learned something about themselves and felt they had
developed on a personal level. They had faced their fears and come
out in one piece.

We weren't sure what to expect from the Dark Copers. After all,
we had only recently discovered this group, and no research had
been conducted on them. Interestingly, the Dark Copers appeared

to get the most out of the experience: They reported feeling great from the rush, much like the Adrenaline Junkies, but they also said they'd learned about themselves and experienced personal development, like the White Knucklers.

We knew some people would get a feel-good rush from the haunt; this was something that had been empirically demonstrated in the past and has historically been the general explanation for why people like horror. However, we were fascinated to find that *many* of the haunted house visitors also reported epistemic benefits from the experience. For them, horror is not just a rush. It's a learning experience, and one that can seemingly have longer-term benefits to personal development.

What kinds of things could someone learn when running through an old fishery with chain-saw-wielding pig-men chasing them? To better understand this, we asked people to elaborate on what they felt they'd learned. Their stories converged around a few themes.

One theme that emerged was the opportunity to face one's fears in the haunt. Before going in, many people were feeling afraid and unsure of themselves. Their minds were on high alert, interpreting their sweaty palms and racing heart as signals of impending danger. However, they mustered up the courage to face their fears with the help of their friends and the playful, safe context of the haunted house. Throughout the experience, these individuals learned that their extreme feelings of fear may have been exaggerated, and that they could handle more than they anticipated.

Another theme revolved around understanding how one reacts in times of stress. Many of us in the modern Western world are lucky enough to rarely be faced with real danger. This is a good thing, but it does mean that when we do find ourselves in danger, we might feel underprepared and paralyzed by fear. By playing with their fear in a safe setting, many of the haunt visitors got a taste of what it's like to *really* feel afraid. They could learn from this high-fear experience because it was couched in a safe and engaging context of play.

Both of these themes, learning what fear feels like and how you handle feeling afraid, map onto the evolutionary function of play. Play evolved because it helped animals safely experience and practice responding to realistic scenarios of high importance. It's an engaging way to practice precarious situations. Children's games like tag and hide-and-seek may seem innocent, but they reveal a darker side if you think carefully about their premise. In hide-and-seek, several kids are hiding while someone is out to get them; in tag, one person is "it" and if they catch you, you lose. When you think about the rules and mechanics of these innocent-looking games, it becomes clear how they simulate dangerous situations in nature. In the case of tag and hide-and-seek, children are engaging in simulations of predator-prey interactions.

FEELING THE FEAR

Using our incredible capacity for imagination, humans can simulate and play with an endless variety of threats. While this in itself is unique among animals, humans can take it even further. We don't just practice specific situations through our simulations; we also practice feeling a certain way and responding to those feelings.

If you are inexperienced at regulating intense negative emotions such as fear or anxiety, it can lead to behaviors that put you in danger or prevent you from resolving conflict. When it comes to feelings of fear and anxiety, there is no better sandbox than horror. For many people, horror media is a safe place for them to challenge themselves or work through difficult emotions. For those people, horror can serve as terrifying therapy.

11.

THE KIDS ARE ALL SPOOKY

Curiosity will conquer fear even more than bravery will.
Indeed, it has led many people into dangers which mere
physical courage would shudder away from.

— *James Stephens's story of "The Coming of Pan" in* The Crock of Gold

A MOST MORBID GAME

I had a summer side job as a traveling "Mad Scientist" while working on my master's degree. I was basically a discount Bill Nye. In addition to my traveling show, I would also lead weeklong science workshops at summer camps. The workshops would last a couple of hours each day and would cover a variety of topics. The kids would engage in hands-on learning in chemistry, biology, forensics, entomology, meteorology, and more.

The kids at the summer camps varied in age, but most were between five and seven years old. If you've ever been around kids that age, you know that their attention span is about as long as a grain of rice, especially when they're at a summer camp with ten or fifteen of their friends. As someone who at that point had taught only college students, I found teaching young kids to be a bit of a learning curve.

My plan was to teach a lesson for maybe half an hour or so and then let the kids play a game or have some free time. This way, I could fit in four or five lessons each day while keeping the kids entertained and engaged.

As a twentysomething with no kids, I didn't know a lot of games that could be played indoors with a group of children. The typical camp classroom was too small for anything like tag or hide-and-seek. Sometimes we would have access to a gym and could play games like capture the flag. However, many of the summer camps didn't have this luxury. This meant that I needed to find something for a group of kids to play in a room the size of a classroom that would keep all of them engaged and entertained. It needed to be something that was easy to learn and easy to play. One game kept coming to mind, but it was a pretty morbid game. However, with my other options exhausted or unavailable, I was running out of ideas.

I gathered the kids after their first lesson of the day and told them we were going to try a game called Mafia. I asked them to grab their chairs and arrange them in a circle. Mafia has several gameplay variations and optional rules. However, the basic gameplay is pretty much the same in all variations. The game centers around a town where there is a small number of killers who secretly murder a townsperson each night. It's the job of the townspeople to figure out who is doing the killing and bring them to justice.

The kids *loved this game*. After they had the hang of the gameplay, I decided to let some of the kids play the part of narrator. The game narration can be as plain or as fantastical as you want, and much of the narrator's imagination comes into play when the town wakes up and the narrator tells the people what happened that night. When I was the narrator, I kept the story as simple and family friendly as I could: "So-and-so was murdered by the mafia last night." I was already worried that I would be getting confused calls from parents whose kids told them they murdered their friends today at mad science camp, so I didn't want to push my luck.

However, my narration was apparently too tame for the children. When the kids started narrating, the game became *much* more morbid. The town quickly descended into chaos and began to resemble scenes from the most terrifying horror movies. Murder weapons became more creative, kills became comically exaggerated, and the townspeople's excitement at hanging the accused each morning was palpable. Young kids were more morbidly curious than I had expected.

WHAT IS CHILDHOOD GOOD FOR?

Humans have an unusually long juvenile period, and children remain dependent upon their caregivers far longer than juveniles in other species. Even among primates, human childhood is peculiar. Rather than transition straight from infancy to middle childhood like other primates, humans have a period of early childhood between ages four and six. During this time, the child's brain continues to grow quickly despite a slowing down of bodily growth. Humans also have an incredibly extended adolescence. Whereas our chimpanzee cousins experience a short one- or two-year period of adolescence, human adolescence lasts between five and eight years.

Childhood is incredibly costly, making the extended human juvenile period an intriguing puzzle for evolutionary scientists. Kids require food, shelter, teaching of social and practical skills, and a decent amount of attention. On top of these needs, they contribute next to nothing to the group's resources.

Childhood also carries with it a remarkably high death rate, or at least it has historically. When you read that human life expectancy has increased dramatically in the past few hundred years, what is often not mentioned is that this increase comes almost entirely from a massive reduction in infant and childhood mortality rates. Of course, lifesaving medicines and increased nutrition have also contributed to people living longer lives. However, the increases in life expectancy that come at the middle and end of life have been a drop in the bucket compared to reductions in infant and childhood mortality.

The current estimate for global infant mortality (dying before age one) is 2.9 percent, whereas childhood mortality (dying before age fifteen) is 4.6 percent. Some countries have pushed their infant and childhood mortality rates even lower. In Iceland, over 99 percent of people survive beyond age fifteen. For most of recorded history, the average infant mortality rate was about 27 percent, while childhood mortality rate was about 46 percent. In other words, only about *half* of all people who were born made it to adulthood. These numbers line up with what we see in modern hunter-gatherer groups, where just under half of those born never make it past age fifteen.

If only half of all people born were making it to reproductive age, that means at least half of all people born were not passing on their genes. This created an incredible evolutionary selection pressure for whatever features in our species keep a child alive long enough to reproduce. Given this selection pressure, it's especially puzzling that humans evolved a childhood that was almost double that of their primate ancestors. Why would we have evolved to increase the time we spend at ages when we are most vulnerable? From an evolutionary point of view, it's safe to assume that this extended childhood must reap enough benefits to offset the baggage of increased energy consumption and risk of mortality that it created.

Psychologist Alison Gopnik has argued that childhood is an adaptation that helps a species solve the explore–exploit dilemma. This refers to the decision one must make to either explore new and unknown aspects of the environment or exploit the aspects with which they are already familiar. We encounter this dilemma all the time. You encountered it the last time you went out for dinner. Did you try a new restaurant or return to one you had been to before and knew you'd enjoy? You encountered this dilemma when you decided to purchase this book. Do you spend time and resources to potentially (hopefully!) learn something new and interesting, or should you save that time and those resources for something you already own?

While we must make these explore–exploit decisions on a daily basis, we tend to have an overarching strategy depending on what life stage we are in. Adults tend to exploit: They use the knowledge and skills they gain throughout life to acquire a steady job that provides a stable source of income. Children tend to explore: They spend most of their time and energy on learning. You can even trace this difference to the brain's caloric consumption. In adults, the brain makes up about 20 percent of the body's resting metabolic rate (calories burned when you're at rest); kids' brains burn through over 50 percent of their resting metabolic rate. Despite the physical energy kids might be known for, the energy consumption of their bodies doesn't hold a candle to that of their growing brains.

This division of labor, where juveniles acquire knowledge and adults provide resources from the knowledge they've acquired, turns out to be a good species-level solution to the explore–exploit dilemma. Although it seems obvious that kids would learn while adults work, it could presumably work the other way around. Children could be running Fortune 500 companies while adults sit in school from 8:00 a.m. to 3:00 p.m. It could also be the case that kids and adults both explore more than they exploit, or vice versa. However, none of these options are as productive as an exploratory childhood and an exploitative adulthood.

THE IMPORTANCE OF PLAY

If childhood is reserved mainly for exploration and adulthood mostly for exploitation, then it follows that a species with a complex adult life would benefit from a longer childhood. A longer childhood allows for more time to explore various aspects of the environment and learn appropriate skills that will be useful in adulthood. At the core of exploration is a drive for playful behavior—an area where children excel over adults.

Frequency and complexity of play are positively correlated with brain size and adult behavioral complexity. More so than many other animals, mammals have big brains and complex behaviors for acquiring food and navigating social life. It's no surprise, then, that play is more common in mammals, particularly among carnivorous mammals. That doesn't mean your pet lizard doesn't engage in some sort of play when it's a juvenile, but its form of play will be much less frequent and more simplistic, perhaps to the point of being unrecognizable. However, it's immediately obvious to us when mammals, such as dogs or cats, are playing. In fact, we often engage in cross-species play with them.

Play serves an important role in training behaviors that are somewhat specific to a species. Lions, tigers, and domesticated cats frequently act stealthy and paw at objects. This playful behavior mimics real-world predation situations for felines. Most big cats stalk their prey, much like your house cat stalks a moth or a mouse. This is why a laser pointer is king when it comes to cat toys. The laser dot resembles a small animal that they can stalk and chase. Felines also excel at catching small prey with their hooked claws. In play, they use pawing motions much more than other mammals. If your cat is anything like mine, it will be more inclined to reach underneath a door to get a toy rather than walk around to the other side.

While felines prefer stealthy ambushes, canids such as wolves, coyotes, and domesticated dogs like to chase. This play behavior mimics the real-world predation techniques that most canids use. Your dog probably does not stalk their plush toy. Instead, they come barreling toward it when they see it or hear it squeak. Unlike felines, canids typically pursue their prey through tracking and subsequent chasing. This is also why dog parks are usually large open spaces; the cat equivalent would require tall grass and plenty of objects and cubbyholes for them to sneak around.

Humans arguably have some of the most complex behaviors among animals for acquiring food. Our modern-day behavior for acquiring food has been drastically simplified to the point of clicking a few buttons on your computer when you see a picture of food that you like. Historically, however, the omnivorous diet of humans has been incredibly complex. Food acquisition in humans can involve hunting, gathering, plant cultivation, and animal husbandry. Making this even more complex, humans don't have a sole source of food to which they are specialized. Our minds and bodies evolved to be flexible when it comes to acquiring and eating food. Sometimes we needed to find a bush of berries that weren't poisonous, and sometimes we needed to kill a mammoth.

As complex as human food acquisition might be, or at least used to be, human social life is many times more complex. No other species comes close to having the complexity of human social life, which includes complex forms of communication through acquired language and all aspects of material and social culture. Making things even more complicated, language and culture can vary immensely between groups of people. The basic units and format of language and culture are similar enough that any human brain is equipped to learn any of them, but their final forms vary widely. So, while we do have psychological mechanisms that have evolved to learn and transmit both language and culture, the exact language we learn and the particular cultural norms we adopt are undetermined at the biological level.

The point of all this is simply to say that (1) play is more common in juvenile developmental periods for species with complex adult behaviors, and (2) humans have extraordinarily complex behaviors as adults. Given this, it makes sense that humans have evolved a longer childhood that allows juveniles more time to play and learn how to be a human adult.

What is more interesting, though, is that kids spend so much of this precious learning time playing with the darker side of life. Villainous characters and dangerous situations are a cornerstone of children's pretend play. When it comes to playing with fear, kids might be more morbidly curious than adults.

PROMOTING SCARY PLAY

Looking back now on how much the summer camp kids enjoyed the game Mafia, I shouldn't have been surprised. In surveys where children are asked about their favorite types of books, ghost stories and horror consistently rank near the top of the list. There's a reason Grimm's Fairy Tales all have spooky elements of danger. Sure, adults might be trying to teach kids important lessons through them, but that doesn't explain why kids like them.

My colleagues at the Recreational Fear Lab conducted a study at Danish schools to better understand scary play among kids. They found that songs of death, torture, and monsters commonly filled the halls of the Danish kindergartens. Other dark games and frightening stories were also common among the children's playtime activities.

One specific example that the researchers wrote about in their study caught my attention. Apparently, one teacher had introduced a game called Werewolf to his students, and the students loved it so much that they demanded to play it almost every day. Werewolf is a card game where a few players have to convince the other players, the townspeople, that they are not werewolves and that they did not kill and eat a townsperson the night before. And the townspeople have to figure out who the werewolves are and kill them.

Sound familiar? That's because Werewolf is a variant of the game Mafia, only with werewolves instead of mafia members.

The Danish schoolteachers who were interviewed spoke positively about the scary play that the kids engaged in during playtime. They thought that scary play was *good* for children's development and not a cause for concern. In fact, many of the teachers felt that it helped children develop emotional skills for dealing with fear, overcoming anxiety, and coping with a loss of control.

These Danish teachers appear to be on to something. One of the most influential evolutionary theories of play argues that play evolved in part to help animals learn how to regain their motor and emotional control in the face of surprises. If an animal is surprised by a stealthy predator, it will be filled with fear and immediately turn to begin running. This is a remarkably disorienting experience unless you've practiced it. The complexity of this maneuver is evident in the flailing movements of baby prey animals such as deer. If you ever watch children play outdoor games, this is exactly the kind of maneuvers they are performing: lots of quick running, turning around, spinning, rolling, jumping, and other activities that cause them to temporarily lose control of their bodily movements and spatial orientation.

Kids play in a variety of ways that induce fear in tolerable levels. This may involve climbing, chasing, sliding, and other physical activities that give them a bit of an adrenaline rush. However, it also often involves scary cognitive play: pretend play with villains, monsters, predators, a floor full of lava, and other kinds of dangers. By introducing scary elements to their games, kids are implicitly practicing feeling afraid and overcoming that fear in pursuit of a goal.

It was good to know I wasn't entirely in the wrong for playing Mafia with the kids, at least in the eyes of Danish schoolteachers. However, not everyone believes in the benefit of spooky things and morbid curiosity when it comes to kids. "Is it okay for my kids to watch scary movies?" is one of the most frequent questions I get. It's a valid concern; some scary stuff is simply too scary for most kids (and some adults, for that matter). However, this doesn't mean that kids should never experience scary stuff. Fortunately for both me and the Danes, the science of scary play points to the benefits of children playing with fear and thrills.

LEARNING TO FACE YOUR FEARS

A lot of people ask me how I got into horror, not just as an academic topic but as a fan. For most people, their introduction to horror was a movie: *Halloween*, *A Nightmare on Elm Street*, and *The Thing* are common answers. I can't remember the first horror movie I saw, though I think it might have been something a bit campy like *Wishmaster* or *Leprechaun*. My real introduction to horror, however, was video games.

My earliest horror genre memory was playing *Resident Evil* on PlayStation 1 when I was about five or six years old. I was probably too young to be playing it—definitely too young according to the Entertainment Software Ratings Board, or ESRB, which gave *Resident Evil* a Mature 17+ rating due to its portrayal of violence, blood, gore, and language. *Resident Evil* was, and still is, terrifying and unforgiving in its gameplay. A mixture of puzzles, zombies, and conspiracies, the game challenges the player's wits and courage.

As a young kid, I found the game incredibly scary. I would often find myself needing to flee to an in-game safe room where I could gather my courage and plan my next move. When I couldn't make it to a safe room or didn't know where the closest one was, I would pause the game to catch my breath and let my heart rate slow down. Despite needing these breaks, I knew I wasn't in any *real* danger; I felt the fear but knew I was safe. The game was also intriguing and challenging enough to keep me coming back for more. It prodded me to face my fears and taught me that I could overcome them. It showed me that even if something was scary, I could conquer my fears and achieve my goals.

While I wouldn't necessarily recommend that people let their five-year-olds play *Resident Evil*, I think it taught me how to better deal with feelings of fear and anxiety. It taught me what those feelings were like in a safe setting and showed me that they didn't have to be immobilizing. Funnily enough, I didn't come to this conclusion until after my scientific research led me to the conclusion that horror might be able to serve this very purpose. Like many other horror fans, I had accidentally discovered that facing fictional fears helped me conquer real fears.

Although your parents may have told you that video games are a waste of time, there is some fascinating research showing that video games can be good for you. In fact, scientists have created a game specifically to help treat anxiety in children. Any guesses on the genre of the game?

That's right, there's a scientifically backed horror survival game that helps treat anxiety in children. The Games for Emotional and Mental Health (GEMH) Lab helped create a game called *Mind-Light*. It follows the story of a young boy named Arty who finds himself in his grandmother's mansion. Unfortunately for Arty, his grandmother's massive house has been taken over by evil, shadowy forces. Playing as Arty, players must bring light back into the house and save his grandmother. Throughout the house, Arty encounters shadowy creatures that block main objectives. The only way to defeat the monsters is by shining a light on them. Luckily, Arty discovers a glowing hat in his bedroom that can be used to shine light on the monsters. Sounds easy enough, right?

But of course, there's a catch. *MindLight* is a biofeedback game

MindLight gameplay.

that incorporates an EEG headband that measures brain waves associated with relaxation. If the player gets too anxious during the game, like when they're facing a shadowy monster, the EEG picks this up and sends a signal to the game that dims the glowing hat (the eponymous mindlight). When the mindlight is too dim, it is no longer powerful enough to defeat the monsters. A visual cue then pops up on the screen that offers tips backed by cognitive behavioral therapy to help the player regain their sense of calm and overcome the feeling of anxiety—like a guided version of me pausing *Resident Evil*.

Once the player reaches a state of relaxation, the mindlight begins to shine brightly again and the player can defeat the shadowy monsters. This serves as psychological reinforcement, teaching the player that calming down in the face of anxiety and fear is a good way to overcome the thing that made them anxious or fearful in the first place. *MindLight* brilliantly utilizes aspects of cognitive behavioral therapy (CBT), exposure therapy, neuroscience, and video game narrative to help treat anxiety. And this works *only* because the game is scary. If the game didn't induce actual feelings of anxiety and fear, the neurofeedback aspect would be rendered irrelevant. In order for them to learn how to overcome fear and anxiety, the children have to play with it.

There are now numerous studies reporting on the efficacy of *MindLight* for treating anxiety in children. For example, one randomized clinical control trial found that *MindLight* was as effective as CBT, the gold standard for treating anxiety. Another study found that more approach-oriented in-game behaviors and fewer avoidant behaviors were key to *MindLight*'s power in reducing anxiety. Children who spent more time exploring the fearful environment had even lower anxiety symptoms at follow-up appointments than children who avoided their fears by hiding in the game. Importantly, this finding held true even when controlling for the children's pregame anxiety levels.

Children also rate *MindLight* as fun, which is more important than it might sound. Although the principles of CBT are scientifically sound, children (and adults, for that matter) don't always find CBT exercises to be fun. This leads to reduced engagement with the practices, decreased motivation to learn, and ultimately a less effective session. By entrenching these principles in a game rather than homework, it creates conditions in which children are much more likely to learn and retain the skills they need to help them deal with anxiety and fear. After all, children are built to play.

THE RISK OF NO RISK

We in the modern Western world are lucky that our children are remarkably safe compared to children in the past. Lions, leopards, wolves, and other predators rarely make snacks out of children these days. Still, nature does not let us rest on our laurels. Children are born with an itch to explore and engage in frightening and thrilling play. This tendency has been crafted through millions of years of natural selection and won't be going away anytime soon. While it may not serve to protect most of us from lions prowling around the savanna today, it could help protect us from an even more terrifying foe: anxiety.

As a kid, I spent a lot of time playing outside. I grew up in a rural area where there was no lack of creeks, forests, canyons, and other places to explore. There often wasn't a purpose to the play; it was just unstructured exploration. This meant I sometimes got a little turned around or found myself in somewhat precarious situations. If I needed to cross a creek, I had to be sure I could make the jump or find a hanging vine that would support my weight to swing across. If I was exploring a canyon, I had to be sure of my footing and make sure what I was standing on was solid. As I walked through forested areas, I had to keep an eye out for snakes or other animals that wouldn't take too kindly to my intrusion.

My playful and exploration-filled childhood was, at times, thrilling, risky, and a bit scary. And it was probably good for me.

Despite it being less than three decades ago, my childhood experience of play would be pretty atypical for many kids who are growing up today. Kids' independence is increasingly strained by shifting cultural values and safety concerns. Unsupervised and unstructured play has been on the decline over the past few decades, which means kids are exposed less to adventurous styles of play that promote thrilling and fun-scary experiences. Situations that would have been considered perfectly normal twenty years ago are now perceived by some as dangerous.

In 2015, a Maryland couple dropped off their children, six and ten, at a local park two blocks from their house. They told the kids to be home by 6:00 p.m. Less than an hour after they were dropped off, the children found themselves sitting in a police car outside of child services. Their crime? Playing unsupervised.

Adventurous and unsupervised play is good for kids. When children engage in this type of play, they are exposed to situations that put them outside of their comfort zone. Climbing trees, jumping off swings, and exploring unfamiliar terrain keep children right on the line of what they are comfortable doing and what they are a bit afraid of doing. As children confront their fears and overcome challenges, they build self-confidence and resilience in stressful situations.

As unsupervised, thrilling play has declined, rates of childhood anxiety have been on the rise. A child today is over five times more likely to be diagnosed with generalized anxiety disorder than they were in the 1950s. This rise in anxiety has been accompanied by decreases in locus of control, which refers to the degree to which you believe you, rather than external factors, are in control of your actions. Play psychologist Peter Gray has argued that our society's decline in unstructured play has left our children with a lack of experience in confronting uncertainty and less likely to have a sense of control over their lives. Locus of control is tightly linked with feelings of anxiety, so it seems plausible, even likely, that low levels of unsupervised and thrilling play could be predisposing many children to increased levels of anxiety.

I hope we can return to a cultural norm where unsupervised and adventurous outdoor play becomes acceptable. Until this happens, however, one possibility in the meantime is to let your child engage in frightening imaginary worlds. Scary fictions are well suited to offer children many of the benefits of risky and thrilling play. Reading a scary book, watching a scary TV show, or playing a scary game allows children the opportunity to safely face the things that frighten them. Scary fictions offer children a productive way to engage with fear and practice those same feelings of uncertainty and anxiety that are present in thrilling and adventurous play. I'm not suggesting that horror fiction should or even can completely replace adventurous outdoor play. However, the very nature of scary fiction offers children exposure to many of the same benefits as other forms of thrilling play. Kids are naturally a little spooky, and we need to let them be spooky.

12.

A MISUNDERSTOOD VIRTUE

*While caution is a useful instinct, we lose many
opportunities and much of the adventure of life if we fail
to support the curious explorer within us.*

—*Joseph Campbell*

NOT EVERYTHING IS WHAT IT SEEMS

Jeffrey Dahmer is one of the most notorious serial killers of all time. As with many serial killers, the public craved information about the circumstances surrounding his life. What did young Dahmer experience early in life that could have led him to murder and cannibalize so many young men? Did his actions as a child or adult give any clues to his evil nature?

There were two aspects of Dahmer's life that captured the public's imagination. The first was that, from a young age, Dahmer had a fascination with bones and dead animals. Dahmer's father, a chemist, noticed his son's morbid fascination after pulling a dead rodent out from under the family home.

In an attempt to bond with his son, Dahmer's father used his knowledge of chemistry to show his son how chemicals could clean and preserve the bones of animals. Dahmer was enthralled by this and developed a passion for collecting and bleaching the bones of roadkill. It was an untraditional father-son activity, for sure, and the morbid nature of Dahmer's childhood curiosity caught the public's attention when it came to light after his arrest.

The second odd aspect of Dahmer's life that the public latched on to was his love of the movie *The Exorcist III*. According to his confession, Dahmer would watch the film several times per week. Even stranger, he would force his victims to watch the movie with him before he murdered them. The strangest part of all is that *The Exorcist III* tells the story of a serial killer who would keep the body parts of his victims, just as Dahmer did.

Dahmer recognized his own morbid curiosity. After he murdered his first victim, he put the body in a crawl space of his grandmother's home. In an interview while he was in prison, Dahmer was asked why he went back to check on the body after hiding it in the crawl space. His answer was simple: morbid curiosity. At one point, Dahmer even stated, "People go to these gory horror movies to get a glimpse of . . . of what they show in the movies. The only difference is, I did it for real."

Dahmer's morbidly curious behavior seemed odd to many. And because it was odd, it stood out to some people as a potential sign of his murderous ways. *Of course* Dahmer dismembered his victims and kept their body parts. Look at how he spent his childhood, collecting roadkill and bleaching bones. And as an adult, he was obsessed with a horror movie about a serial killer! That must have been a sign of his inner killer, right?

Many people had similar thoughts about violent video games in the late 1990s and early 2000s. Video games were becoming much more realistic, and many parents and politicians were increasingly concerned about their effects on young, impressionable minds. Psychologists made entire careers out of studying the effects of violent video games on children. Worries were at an all-time high by the end of the century. Then, in 1999, two students at Columbine High School shot and killed twelve of their classmates and a teacher and injured over twenty others before taking their own lives. Understandably, the nation wanted answers.

As with Dahmer's gruesome crimes, the public was shocked and searched for clues to explain the Columbine shooters' actions. How could these two kids have committed such terrible crimes? What would have driven them to this? Was it something in their home life? Were there any signs of their inner demons?

Rumors began to spread soon after the shooting. As so often is the case, many were false, but some had an element of truth. One of the rumors that was true was that the two Columbine shooters loved video games, particularly the violent first-person shooter *Doom* and the gruesome fighting game *Mortal Kombat*. And there it was. The public had found their answer to what made these kids so violent. In many people's eyes, the violent nature of the shooters was a consequence of their morbid curiosity.

Morbid curiosity has long been a scapegoat for bad behavior. An interest in or curiosity about bodily injuries, violence, demons, or dangerous men will be a sign to many people that something is wrong. Of course, this brings up an ironic conundrum: Those who were interested in gathering facts about what made killers like Jeffrey Dahmer or the Columbine High School shooters violent were *also* engaging their morbid curiosity. If morbid curiosity made Dahmer a murderous cannibal and two kids from Columbine High School mass shooters, why didn't it also contaminate the minds of the millions who were curious about the psychology and behaviors of these dangerous men?

The answer is simple: Dahmer was not a murderous cannibal because of his morbid curiosity. The Columbine shooters did not murder their classmates because they played *Mortal Kombat* and *Doom*. And the people who were curious enough to investigate the details surrounding the lives of these murderers were not going to become violent as a consequence of their morbid curiosity.

Dahmer had many other things going on that may have contributed to his murderous ways. He himself claimed that he didn't want to kill his victims, but that killing them was one way to ensure they would not leave him. Dahmer thought that he might be able to induce a zombified state in them by drilling holes in their skulls and pouring acid on their brains. When this didn't work and the victims succumbed to their wounds or were otherwise killed by Dahmer, he would keep their body parts as a way to keep the individuals with him. His kidnappings and killings were driven by psychopathology, not his morbid curiosity.

Less is known about the Columbine shooters since they were underage at the time of their crimes and died by suicide before they could be interrogated. However, family and classmates have said that they were targets of bullying, were quick to anger, and had self-destructive personalities. We will likely never know why they did what they did. But we can be pretty certain that it had nothing to do with the types of video games they enjoyed.

Doom and *Mortal Kombat* are violent games, but violent games do not make violent people. Millions of kids play violent video games without any instances of violent aggression. Thousands of academic articles over several years have failed to find a consistent effect of violent video games on violent behavior. About 20 percent of school shooters (nearly 100 percent of whom are male) played violent video games. However, *70 percent* of male high school students play violent video games. Statistically, kids who shoot up schools are *less* likely to play violent video games. This isn't because playing violent video games prevents you from becoming a school shooter, either. Instead, the most straightforward interpretation is that morbid curiosity is a typical part of human behavior and is largely unrelated to committing violent acts.

HARNESSING THE BEAST

Morbid curiosity is infused throughout human life. It's not just about craning your neck as you drive by the car wreck or going to see the newest horror flick in theaters. Morbid curiosity is an adaptive behavior that is central to the success of our species. It helped our ancestors understand, cope with, and survive the dangers of their environment. It fueled their imagination and inspired stories of menacing predators, local legends, healing remedies, fairy tales, and dangerous monsters and murderers in their dreams.

But morbid curiosity isn't just a relic of our ancestors who lived in harsh and unforgiving environments. Our taste for the macabre can still serve us well today if we learn to harness it. Mastering the darker grooves of our mind can help us live rich, authentic lives and overcome our fears.

Many people shut out the negative side of life. They try to hide anything related to fear, disgust, or anxiety behind tightly sealed doors in their minds. Being open to experiencing these emotions in safe contexts prevents us from being naïve to their effects. Feeling afraid or anxious can catch us off guard and leave us ill-equipped to handle the situations that precipitate those emotions. But if we are practiced in dealing with these emotions, we can more expertly navigate them. A true crime documentary, oddities festival, or haunted attraction can evoke these feelings in a safe setting, allow us to play with these internal signals of danger, and help us become more familiar with them. When we open the door to safe experiences with bad feelings, we can more easily conquer them.

Some people even live out their morbid curiosity through their careers. Think of the most morbidly curious professions: Which ones come to mind? Doctors, nurses, military professionals, and criminal profilers are all a bit more morbidly curious than the average Joe. But one career in particular stands out as a strong candidate for the most morbidly curious: the mortuary and funeral profession.

It's clear from the scientific literature and perhaps from your own personal experience that personality influences career choice. Cosmetologists are extraverted, athletes are risk-takers, musicians and artists are high in openness to experience, and midwives are conscientious. To embalm, cremate, and otherwise work with dead bodies, you must be motivated by morbid curiosity to some extent.

The macabre nature of the funerary profession has caught the attention of existential psychologists, who are interested in how people can live authentic and fulfilling lives. Is it possible to live a good life when you are surrounded by death nearly every day? To investigate this, a team of existential psychologists examined the personality features that are most typical in funeral professionals.

Funeral professionals exhibit a number of traits associated with authentic living. One of those is psychological flexibility: The ability to power through unpleasant thoughts, feelings, and experiences in pursuit of a goal. Those who work in the death industry have higher levels of this trait than those who are not in the death industry. Funeral workers also have lower levels of death anxiety and less avoidant coping styles. When faced with a frightening challenge, they are more likely to approach and solve the issue than avoid the issue and suppress their feelings. Like other morbidly curious people, funeral workers have safely exposed themselves to the darker side of life, building their resilience to challenging and chilling scenarios.

YOUR MORBIDLY CURIOUS LEGACY

You are part of an unbroken line of organisms who have effectively evaded predation for over five hundred million years. From the earliest organisms who escaped their ocean predators with primitive eyespots to Ice Age humans whose vivid imaginations led them to draw menacing lions on the walls of caves, morbid curiosity kept our ancestors out of the jaws of the creatures that hunted them. Your ancestors have passed on to you a curiosity for the dark side of life, that itch you have to peek when you're not sure if you should.

Now that we live in a safer world than any of our ancestors could have ever dreamed, the benefits of being morbidly curious may seem less obvious. However, it still motivates us to face the parts of life that we are sometimes afraid to experience. It gives us the push we sometimes need to play with fear and explore our anxiety. In doing this, we develop confidence that we can overcome the challenges that life throws at us, and we prepare our mind for the difficult and dangerous times that we will inevitably face.

ACKNOWLEDGMENTS

The final pages of a book are simply the record of a longer process that involves a lot of thinking and discussing ideas with others. I'll do my best here to thank those whose ideas, time, and support were instrumental in producing this book.

I was lucky enough to develop an area of expertise during my PhD that I truly enjoyed. I want to thank my adviser, Dario Maestripieri, for giving me the freedom during graduate school to pursue my interests and develop that expertise. He also offered me a wealth of useful advice that helped me navigate the early months of pitching my book.

This book, and much of my research program, would not exist if it wasn't for Mathias Clasen's consistent support of my work. Mathias has been my most reliable and important collaborator for many years, and I've been lucky to have him in my corner. From makeshift labs at haunted houses to my dissertation defense, he has influenced my research more than any other scholar.

Thanks as well to the other members of my dissertation committee who gave critical feedback on the scientific portion of this project: Marc G. Berman, Richard Shweder, and Stephen T. Asma.

I also want to thank my agent, Max Brockman. I feel lucky to be among the many inspiring and successful scientists who he represents. Special thanks as well to Rob K. Henderson for introducing us.

I want to thank Connor Brown at Viking for being the first person to encourage me to seriously consider writing a book about my research. Thanks also to my acquiring editor, Matthew Klise, for seeing the potential in this book very early on.

Thank you to those who took the time to read over various chapter drafts and offer feedback: A. C. Harkness, Angelina Vasquez, Benjamin van Buren, Bryce Huebner, Eric Shattuck, James O'Loughlin, Jason Just, Lilian Carvalho, Luke Smith, Marco Varella, Matthew Kressin, Merrick Powell, Paola Baca, Rob Sica, Shanley Weston, Valerie van Mulukom, Will Harrison, and Xavier Bonilla.

Special thanks to Amanda Moran for her support while I was writing this book, and for her thoughtful feedback throughout several stages of the manuscript. Thanks also to my family and friends for their support over the past few years.

Finally, I want to thank Camille LeBlanc, whose editorial shrewdness helped me craft a book that I can be proud of.

NOTES

PROLOGUE

1 Fans of *Saw*: Johnny Oleksinski, "'Spiral' Signals the Death of 'Torture Porn'—Good Riddance!," *New York Post*, May 13, 2021, nypost.com/2021/05/13/spiral-signals-the-death-of-torture-porn-good-riddance.

2 *Friday the 13th* was a success: "Friday the 13th (1980)," The Numbers, the-numbers.com/movie/Friday-the-13th-(1980).

2 In his review of: Gene Siskel, "'Friday the 13th': More Bad Luck," *Chicago Tribune*, May 12, 1980, newspapers.com/article/chicago-tribune-gene-siskel-movie-review/87596741.

2 Siskel speculated that: Roger Ebert and Gene Siskel, "Extreme Violence Directed at Women," *Sneak Previews*, season 5, episode 4, aired 1980 on PBS.

CHAPTER ONE: WHY WE CAN'T LOOK AWAY

13 Psychologists have long: Paul Rozin and Edward B. Royzman, "Negativity Bias, Negativity Dominance, and Contagion," *Personality and Social Psychology Review* 5, no. 4 (2001): 296–320, doi.org/10.1207/s15327957pspr0504_2.

14 As social psychologist: Roy F. Baumeister et al., "Bad Is Stronger Than Good," *Review of General Psychology* 5, no. 4 (2001): 323–70, doi.org/10.1037/1089-2680.5.4.323.

14 Threat-related information is seen: Pascal Boyer and Nora Parren, "Threat-Related Information Suggests Competence: A Possible Factor in the Spread of Rumors," *PLOS ONE* 10, no. 6 (2015): e0128421, doi.org/10.1371/journal.pone.0128421.

15 Boyer and his: Timothy Blaine and Pascal Boyer, "Origins of Sinister Rumors: A Preference for Threat-Related Material in the Supply and Demand of Information," *Evolution and Human Behavior* 39, no. 1 (2017): 67–75, doi.org/10.1016/j.evolhumbehav.2017.10.001.

16 Our sensitivity to threat-related: Randolph M. Nesse, "The Smoke Detector Principle," *Annals of the New York Academy of Sciences* 935, no. 1 (2001): 75–85, doi.org/10.1111/j.1749-6632.2001.tb03472.x.

17 Psychologists John Tierney: John Tierney and Roy F. Baumeister, *The Power* *of Bad: How the Negativity Effect Rules Us and How We Can Rule It* (Penguin Press, 2019).

19 In a study that: H. Clark Barrett and James Broesch, "Prepared Social Learning About Dangerous Animals in Children," *Evolution and Human Behavior* 33, no. 5 (2012): 499–508, doi.org/10.1016/j.evolhumbehav.2012.01.003.

22 We have managed: Michelle Scalise Sugiyama, "Lions and Tigers and Bears: Predators as a Folklore Universal," in *Anthropology and Social History: Heuristics in the Study of Literature,* eds. Hans Friedrich, Fotis Jannidis, Ulrich Klein, Kai Mellmann, Steffen Metzger, and Marcus Willems (Mentis Verlag, 2006).

23 These nuggets of: Michelle Scalise Sugiyama, "Predation, Narration, and Adaptation: 'Little Red Riding Hood' Revisited," *Interdisciplinary Literary Studies* 5, no. 2 (2004): 108–27, jstor.org/stable/41207031.

25 Wes Craven, who: William Schoell and James Spencer, *The Nightmare Never Ends: The Official History of Freddy Krueger and the Nightmare on Elm Street Films* (Citadel Press, 1992).

CHAPTER TWO: THE EVOLUTION OF A MORBIDLY CURIOUS CREATURE

29 Zoologist Andrew Parker: Andrew Parker, *In the Blink of an Eye: How Vision Kick-Started the Big Bang of Evolution,* revised ed. (Simon & Schuster, 2016).

30 Studies with humans: D. Regan and K. I. Beverley, "Looming Detectors in the Human Visual Pathway," *Vision Research* 18, no. 4 (1978): 415–21, doi.org/10.1016/0042-6989(78)90051-2.

30 A similar bias: Robert Baumgartner et al., "Asymmetries in Behavioral and Neural Responses to Spectral Cues Demonstrate the Generality of Auditory Looming Bias," *Proceedings of the National Academy of Sciences* 114, no. 36 (2017): 9743–48, doi.org/10.1073/pnas.1703247114.

31 Prey animals gather: Lee A. Dugatkin and Jean-Guy J. Godin, "Prey Approaching Predators: A Cost-Benefit Perspective," *Annales Zoologici Fennici* 29, no. 4 (1992): 233–52, jstor.org/stable/23735625.

32 Prey observe their: Grant E. Brown and Jean-Guy J. Godin, "Who Dares, Learns: Chemical Inspection Behaviour and Acquired Predator Recognition in a Characin Fish," *Animal Behaviour* 57, no. 2 (1999): 475–81, doi.org/10.1006/anbe.1998.1017; Michael A. Fishman, "Predator Inspection: Closer Approach as a Way to Improve Assessment of Potential Threats," *Journal of Theoretical Biology* 196, no. 2 (1999): 225–35, doi.org/10.1006/jtbi.1998.0834; M. A. Häberli, P. B. Aeschlimann, and M. Milinski, "Sticklebacks Benefit from Closer Predator Inspection: An Experimental Test of Risk Assessment," *Ethology Ecology & Evolution* 17, no. 3 (2005): 249–59, doi.org/10.1080/08927014.2005.9522595.

32 Zoologist Clare FitzGibbon: Clare D. FitzGibbon, "The Costs and Benefits of Predator Inspection Behaviour in Thomson's Gazelles," *Behavioral Ecology and Sociobiology* 34, no. 2 (1994): 139–48, doi.org/10.1007/bf00164184.

34 When you perceive: Joseph E. LeDoux and Daniel Pine, "Using Neuroscience to Help Understand Fear and Anxiety: A Two-System Framework," *American Journal of Psychiatry* 173, no. 11 (2016): 1083–93, doi.org/10.1176/appi.ajp.2016.160 30353.

34 Defending against threats: Joseph E. LeDoux, "As Soon as There Was Life, There Was Danger: The Deep History of Survival Behaviours and the Shallower History of Consciousness," *Philosophical Transactions of the Royal Society B* 377, no. 1844 (2022): 20210292, doi.org/10.1098/rstb.2021.0292.

35 Due to a rare: R. Adolphs et al., "Impaired Recognition of Emotion in Facial Expressions Following Bilateral Damage to the Human Amygdala," *Nature* 372, no. 6507 (1994): 669–72, doi.org/10.1038/372669a0.

35 Scientists have discovered: R. Adolphs et al., "Fear and the Human Amygdala," *Journal of Neuroscience* 15, no. 9 (1995): 5879–91, doi.org/10.1523/jneurosci.15-09 -05879.1995; Ralph Adolphs, Daniel Tranel, and Antonio R. Damasio, "The Human Amygdala in Social Judgment," *Nature* 393, no. 6684 (1998): 470–74, doi .org/10.1038/30982; Antoine Bechara et al., "Double Dissociation of Conditioning and Declarative Knowledge Relative to the Amygdala and Hippocampus in Humans," *Science* 269, no. 5227 (1995): 1115–18, doi.org/10.1126/science .7652558.

35 While investigating her: Justin S. Feinstein et al., "The Human Amygdala and the Induction and Experience of Fear," *Current Biology* 21, no. 1 (2010): 34–38, doi.org/10.1016/j.cub.2010.11.042.

35 To better understand how: Feinstein et al., "The Human Amygdala and the Induction and Experience of Fear."

36 The researchers also: Feinstein et al., "The Human Amygdala and the Induction and Experience of Fear."

37 Humans are experts: Thomas Suddendorf and Michael C. Corballis, "The Evolution of Foresight: What Is Mental Time Travel, and Is It Unique to Humans?" *Behavioral and Brain Sciences* 30, no. 3 (2007): 299–313, doi.org/10.1017/S0140525 X07001975.

37 When imagination enters: Adam Bulley, Julie D. Henry, and Thomas Suddendorf, "Thinking About Threats: Memory and Prospection in Human Threat Management," *Consciousness and Cognition* 49 (2017): 53–69, doi.org/10.1016/j .concog.2017.01.005.

38 Moreover, we tend: Daniel M. T. Fessler, Anne C. Pisor, and Carlos David Navarrete, "Negatively-Biased Credulity and the Cultural Evolution of Beliefs," *PLOS ONE* 9, no. 4 (2014): e95167, doi.org/10.1371/journal.pone.0095167.

38 In many ways, our: Mathias Clasen, "Monsters Evolve: A Biocultural Approach to Horror Stories," *Review of General Psychology* 16, no. 2 (2012): 222–29, doi.org /10.1037/a0027918; Coltan Scrivner and Mathias Clasen, "Why Frightening Imaginary Worlds? Morbid Curiosity and the Learning Potential of Horror," *Behavioral and Brain Sciences* 45 (2022): e315, doi.org/10.1017/S0140525X210 02259.

CHAPTER THREE: MALEFICENT MINDS

39 In the fall of 1991: Jennifer Nalewicki, "Ötzi the Iceman: What We Know 3 Decades After His Discovery," *National Geographic*, February 23, 2021, national geographic.com/science/article/oetzi-the-iceman-what-we-know-3 -decades-after-his-discovery.

40 He had a cloak: "Ötzi's Clothing," South Tyrol Museum of Archaeology, 2016, iceman.it/en/clothing.

41 Then, a new X-ray: Paul Gostner and Eduard Egarter Vigl, "INSIGHT: Report of Radiological-Forensic Findings on the Iceman," *Journal of Archaeological Science* 29, no. 3 (2002): 323–26, doi.org/10.1006/jasc.2002.0824.

41 Ötzi had the blood: Andrew Curry, "Iceman Fights Back," *Science* 375, no. 6583 (2022): 703–7, doi.org/10.1126/science.ada4914.

42 Evolutionary anthropologist Sarah: Sarah Blaffer Hrdy, *Mothers and Others: The Evolutionary Origins of Mutual Understanding* (Harvard University Press, 2011).

43 Chimpanzees, like many: Frans de Waal, *Chimpanzee Politics: Power and Sex Among Apes* (Johns Hopkins University Press, 2007).

43 Biological anthropologist Richard: Richard W. Wrangham, *The Goodness Paradox: The Strange Relationship Between Virtue and Violence in Human Evolution* (Pantheon Books, 2019).

43 What's more, Wrangham: Richard W. Wrangham, "Targeted Conspiratorial Killing, Human Self-Domestication and the Evolution of Groupishness," *Evolutionary Human Sciences* 3 (2021), doi.org/10.1017/ehs.2021.20.

43 The answer lies: Julia C. Babcock et al., "Similarities and Differences in Impulsive/Premeditated and Reactive/Proactive Bimodal Classifications of Aggression," *Aggression and Violent Behavior* 19, no. 3 (2014): 251–62, doi.org/10.1016 /j.avb.2014.04.002; Adrian Raine et al., "The Reactive–Proactive Aggression Questionnaire: Differential Correlates of Reactive and Proactive Aggression in Adolescent Boys," *Aggressive Behavior* 32, no. 2 (2006): 159–71, doi.org/10.1002 /ab.20115; Naomi J. Weinshenker and Allan Siegel, "Bimodal Classification of Aggression: Affective Defense and Predatory Attack," *Aggression and Violent Behavior* 7, no. 3 (2002): 237–50, doi.org/10.1016/s1359-1789(01)00042-8.

44 Although social and: Richard W. Wrangham, "Two Types of Aggression in Human Evolution," *Proceedings of the National Academy of Sciences* 115, no. 2 (2017): 245–53, doi.org/10.1073/pnas.1713611115.

44 In one study, Raine: Adrian Raine et al., "Reduced Prefrontal and Increased Subcortical Brain Functioning Assessed Using Positron Emission Tomography in Predatory and Affective Murderers," *Behavioral Sciences & the Law* 16, no. 3 (1998): 319–32, doi.org/10.1002/(sici)1099-0798(199822)16:3<319::aid-bsl311>3.0.co;2-g.

45 Because proactive aggression: R. J. Blair, "The Neurobiology of Impulsive Aggression," *Journal of Child Psychology and Psychiatry* 57, no. 3 (2016): 282–305, doi .org/10.1089/cap.2015.0088.

47 **Psychologist David Buss:** David M. Buss, *The Murderer Next Door: Why the Mind Is Designed to Kill* (Penguin, 2005).

48 **One of the early:** Joy Wiltenburg, "True Crime: The Origins of Modern Sensationalism," *American Historical Review* 109, no. 5 (2004): 1377–1404, doi.org/10.1086/ahr/109.5.1377.

49 **This more psychologically:** Wiltenburg, "True Crime."

50 **In the 1970s:** Harold Schechter, *The Serial Killer Files: The Who, What, Where, How, and Why of the World's Most Terrifying Murderers* (Ballantine Books, 2003).

51 **John Wayne Gacy:** Peter Vronsky, *American Serial Killers: The Epidemic Years 1950–2000* (Berkley, 2021).

52 **Out of fear:** Barry Strauss, *The Death of Caesar: The Story of History's Most Famous Assassination* (Simon & Schuster, 2015).

53 **In its most basic:** Karen M. Douglas and Robbie M. Sutton, "What Are Conspiracy Theories? A Definitional Approach to Their Correlates, Consequences, and Communication," *Annual Review of Psychology* 74 (2023): 271–98, doi.org/10.1146/annurev-psych-032420-031329.

CHAPTER FOUR: PARANORMAL PERCEPTIONS

55 **Savannah was a major:** Buddy Sullivan, "Atlantic Slave Trade to Savannah," *New Georgia Encyclopedia*, last modified December 17, 2020, georgiaencyclopedia.org/articles/history-archaeology/atlantic-slave-trade-to-savannah.

55 **It was hit:** Robert L. Usinger, "Yellow Fever from the Viewpoint of Savannah," *Georgia Historical Quarterly* 28, no. 3 (1944): 187–203, jstor.org/stable/40576943.

55 **If war, slavery:** Michele Nicole Johnson, "1893 Sea Islands Hurricane," *New Georgia Encyclopedia*, last modified July 8, 2005, georgiaencyclopedia.org/articles/geography-environment/1893-sea-islands-hurricane.

60 **The researchers conducted:** Jesse M. Bering et al., "The 'Ghost' in the Lab: Believers' and Non-Believers' Implicit Responses to an Alleged Apparition," *International Journal for the Psychology of Religion* 32, no. 3 (2021): 214–31, doi.org/10.1080/10508619.2021.1975400.

62 **According to a Gallup:** David W. Moore, "Three in Four Americans Believe in Paranormal," Gallup, June 16, 2005, news.gallup.com/poll/16915/three-four-americans-believe-paranormal.aspx.

63 **He has argued:** Justin L. Barrett, "Exploring the Natural Foundations of Religion," *Trends in Cognitive Sciences* 4, no. 1 (2000): 29–34, doi.org/10.1016/S1364-6613(99)01419-9.

64 **Marc Andersen and his:** Marc Andersen et al., "Agency Detection in Predictive Minds: A Virtual Reality Study," *Religion, Brain & Behavior* 9, no. 1 (2017): 52–64, doi.org/10.1080/2153599x.2017.1378709.

67 **This is known as theory:** Martin Brüne and Ute Brüne-Cohrs, "Theory of Mind—Evolution, Ontogeny, Brain Mechanisms and Psychopathology," *Neuroscience &*

Biobehavioral Reviews 30, no. 3 (2006): 437–55, doi.org/10.1016/j.neubiorev.2005.08.001.

67 **This is key:** Uta Frith and Christopher D. Frith, "Development and Neurophysiology of Mentalizing," *Philosophical Transactions of the Royal Society B* 358, no. 1431 (2003): 459–73, doi.org/10.1098/rstb.2002.1218.

67 **Interestingly, these same:** Harriet Cullen et al., "Individual Differences in Anthropomorphic Attributions and Human Brain Structure," *Social Cognitive and Affective Neuroscience* 9, no. 9 (2013): 1276–80, doi.org/10.1093/scan/nst109.

67 **Developmental psychologist Masako:** Masako Myowa-Yamakoshi, Céline Scola, and Satoshi Hirata, "Humans and Chimpanzees Attend Differently to Goal-Directed Actions," *Nature Communications* 3, no. 1 (2012), doi.org/10.1038/ncomms1695.

68 **Our inclination to look:** Sarah-Jayne Blakemore and Jean Decety, "From the Perception of Action to the Understanding of Intention," *Nature Reviews Neuroscience* 2, no. 8 (2001): 561–67, doi.org/10.1038/35086023.

68 **This tendency to:** Fritz Heider and Marianne Simmel, "An Experimental Study of Apparent Behavior," *American Journal of Psychology* 57, no. 2 (1944): 243, doi.org/10.2307/1416950.

69 **The visual input:** H. Clark Barrett et al., "Accurate Judgments of Intention from Motion Cues Alone: A Cross-Cultural Study," *Evolution and Human Behavior* 26, no. 4 (2005): 313–31, doi.org/10.1016/j.evolhumbehav.2004.08.015.

69 **The assumption that:** Aaron D. Lightner and Edward H. Hagen, "All Models Are Wrong, and Some Are Religious: Supernatural Explanations as Abstract and Useful Falsehoods About Complex Realities," *Human Nature* 33, no. 4 (2022): 425–62, doi.org/10.1007/s12110-022-09437-9.

70 **Because threat-related information:** Pascal Boyer, "Deriving Features of Religions in the Wild: How Communication and Threat-Detection May Predict Spirits, Gods, Witches, and Shamans," *Human Nature* 32, no. 4 (2021): 528–50, doi.org/10.1007/s12110-021-09410-y; Manvir Singh, "Magic, Explanations, and Evil: The Origins and Design of Witches and Sorcerers," *Current Anthropology* 62, no. 1 (2021): 2–29, doi.org/10.1086/713111.

70 **A team of psychologists:** Joshua Conrad Jackson et al., "Supernatural Explanations Across 114 Societies Are More Common for Natural Than Social Phenomena," *Nature Human Behaviour* 7, no. 5 (2023): 707–17, doi.org/10.1038/s41562-023-01558-0.

72 **However, he maintained:** Alma Gottlieb, *The Afterlife Is Where We Come From* (University of Chicago Press, 2015).

73 **One study found that nearly 20 percent:** Mark Ziemann, Yotam Eren, and Assam El-Osta, "Gene Name Errors Are Widespread in the Scientific Literature," *Genome Biology* 17, no. 177 (2016), doi.org/10.1186/s13059-016-1044-7.

CHAPTER FIVE: VICARIOUS VIOLENCE

78 As a compromise: Dana Forsythe, "How *Mortal Kombat*'s Super Nintendo Debut Changed Video Games Forever," *Syfy Wire*, June 10, 2019, syfy.com/syfy-wire/how -mortal-kombats-super-nintendo-debut-changed-video-games-forever.

79 The conclusion of: Aaron Drummond, James D. Sauer, and Christopher J. Ferguson, "Do Longitudinal Studies Support Long-Term Relationships Between Aggressive Game Play and Youth Aggressive Behaviour? A Meta-Analytic Examination," *Royal Society Open Science* 7, no. 7 (2020): 200373, doi.org/10.1098 /rsos.200373; Christopher J. Ferguson, "The Good, the Bad and the Ugly: A Meta-Analytic Review of Positive and Negative Effects of Violent Video Games," *Psychiatric Quarterly* 78, no. 4 (2007): 309–16, doi.org/10.1007/s11126-007-9056-9; Patrick M. Markey and Christopher J. Ferguson, *Moral Combat: Why the War on Violent Video Games Is Wrong* (BenBella Books, 2017); David Trend, *The Myth of Media Violence: A Critical Introduction* (Wiley-Blackwell, 2007).

80 On a busy day: Amanda Claridge, Judith Toms, and Tony Cubberley, *Rome: An Oxford Archaeological Guide* (Oxford University Press, 2010).

80 Although many gladiators: Garrett G. Fagan, *The Lure of the Arena: Social Psychology and the Crowd at the Roman Games* (Cambridge University Press, 2011).

81 However, evolution has: Jerome H. Barkow, Leda Cosmides, and John Tooby, *The Adapted Mind: Evolutionary Psychology and the Generation of Culture* (Oxford University Press, 1995).

81 Many young mammals: Owen Aldis, *Play Fighting* (Elsevier, 2013).

81 Wars, skirmishes, and: Lawrence H. Keeley, *War Before Civilization* (Oxford University Press, 1997).

82 By playing these: Michelle Scalise Sugiyama, Marcela Mendoza, and Lawrence Sugiyama, "War Games: Intergroup Coalitional Play Fighting as a Means of Comparative Coalition Formidability Assessment," *Evolutionary Behavioral Sciences* 15, no. 2 (2021): 91–110, doi.org/10.1037/ebs0000251; Michelle Scalise Sugiyama et al., "Coalitional Play Fighting and the Evolution of Coalitional Intergroup Aggression," *Human Nature* 29, no. 3 (2018): 219–44, doi.org/10.1007 /s12110-018-9319-1.

82 The researchers identified: Anne Bartsch et al., "More Than Shoot-Em-Up and Torture Porn: Reflective Appropriation and Meaning-Making of Violent Media Content," *Journal of Communication* 66, no. 5 (2016): 741–65, doi.org/10 .1111/jcom.12248.

84 The three reflective: Coltan Scrivner, "The Psychology of Morbid Curiosity: Development and Initial Validation of the Morbid Curiosity Scale," *Personality and Individual Differences* 183 (2021): 111139, doi.org/10.1016/j.paid.2021 .111139.

85 One of the first: Coltan Scrivner et al., "Violence Reduces Attention to Faces and Draws Attention to Points of Contact," *Scientific Reports* 9, no. 1 (2019), doi .org/10.1038/s41598-019-54327-3.

86 **It's a common:** R. Brian Ferguson, "War Before Civilization: The Myth of the Peaceful Savage," *American Anthropologist* 99, no. 2 (1997): 424–25, doi.org/10 .1525/aa.1997.99.2.424.

86 **In the US, cities:** *WorldAtlas*, "The Most Dangerous Cities in the World," last modified 2023, worldatlas.com/cities/the-most-dangerous-cities-in-the-world.html.

86 **This is far above:** National Center for Health Statistics, *Assault or Homicide* (Centers for Disease Control and Prevention, 2023), cdc.gov/nchs/fastats/homicide .htm.

87 **Pinker outlines hundreds:** Steven Pinker, *The Better Angels of Our Nature: Why Violence Has Declined* (Viking, 2011).

87 **Still, over 10 percent of deaths:** Pinker, *The Better Angels of Our Nature.*

88 **Just as their model:** José María Gómez et al., "The Phylogenetic Roots of Human Lethal Violence," *Nature* 538, no. 7624 (2016): 233–37, doi.org/10.1038 /nature19758.

88 **It may seem small:** World Health Organization, *The Top 10 Causes of Death* (2020), who.int/news-room/fact-sheets/detail/the-top-10-causes-of-death.

89 **Large canine teeth:** J. Michael Plavcan, "Sexual Size Dimorphism, Canine Dimorphism, and Male-Male Competition in Primates: Where Do Humans Fit In?" *Human Nature* 23, no. 1 (2012): 45–67, doi.org/10.1007/s12110-012-9130-3; J. Michael Plavcan and Carel P. van Schaik, "Intrasexual Competition and Canine Dimorphism in Anthropoid Primates," *American Journal of Physical Anthropology* 87, no. 4 (1992): 461–77, doi.org/10.1002/ajpa.1330870407.

89 **They have a variety:** Samuel D. Gosling and Oliver P. John, "Personality Dimensions in Nonhuman Animals," *Current Directions in Psychological Science* 8, no. 3 (1999): 69–75, doi.org/10.1111/1467-8721.00017.

90 **For many people across:** Alan Page Fiske and Tage Shakti Rai, *Virtuous Violence* (Cambridge University Press, 2015).

91 **The ranking of:** G. A. Parker, "Assessment Strategy and the Evolution of Fighting Behaviour," *Journal of Theoretical Biology* 47, no. 1 (1974): 223–43, doi.org/10 .1016/0022-5193(74)90111-8.

91 **Many times, these:** J. Maynard Smith and George R. Price, "The Logic of Animal Conflict," *Nature* 246, no. 5427 (1973): 15–18, doi.org/10.1038/246015a0.

CHAPTER SIX: INTRIGUING INJURIES

94 **The average time:** Blair Davis and Kial Natale, "The Pound of Flesh Which I Demand: American Horror Cinema, Gore, and the Box Office, 1998–2007," in *American Horror Film: The Genre at the Turn of the Millennium*, ed. Steffen Hantke (University Press of Mississippi, 2010).

95 **Master of horror Stephen:** Stephen King, *Danse Macabre* (Simon & Schuster, 2011).

95 **The *Terror* is related:** H. P. Lovecraft, "Supernatural Horror in Literature" (1927), hplovecraft.com/writings/texts/essays/shil.aspx.

98 However, we aren't: Rita Dolce, *Losing One's Head in the Ancient Near East: Interpretation and Meaning of Decapitation* (Routledge, 2017); Renato Rosaldo, *Ilongot Headhunting, 1883–1974: A Study in Society and History* (Stanford University Press, 1980).

99 One reason a killer: John Thrasher and Toby Handfield, "Honor and Violence: An Account of Feuds, Duels, and Honor Killings," *Human Nature* 29, no. 4 (2018): 371–89, https://doi.org/10.1007/s12110-018-9324-4.

99 Body size reliably: John Archer, *The Behavioural Biology of Aggression* (Cambridge University Press, 1988); Neil R. Caton et al., "Human Male Body Size Predicts Increased Knockout Power, Which Is Accurately Tracked by Conspecific Judgments of Male Dominance," *Human Nature* 35, no. 2 (2024): 114–33, doi.org/10.1007/s12110-024-09473-7.

100 Evolutionary anthropologist Dan Fessler: Daniel M. T. Fessler and Colin Holbrook, "Bound to Lose: Physical Incapacitation Increases the Conceptualized Size of an Antagonist in Men," *PLOS ONE* 8 (2013): e71306, doi.org/10.1371/journal.pone.0071306; Daniel M. T. Fessler and Colin Holbrook, "Marching into Battle: Synchronized Walking Diminishes the Conceptualized Formidability of an Antagonist in Men," *Biology Letters* 10 (2014): 20140592, doi.org/10.1098/rsbl.2014.0592; Daniel M. T. Fessler and Colin Holbrook, "Synchronized Behavior Increases Assessments of the Formidability and Cohesion of Coalitions," *Evolution and Human Behavior* 37, no. 6 (2016): 502–9, doi.org/10.1016/j.evolhumbehav.2016.05.003; Daniel M. T. Fessler et al., "Foundations of the Crazy Bastard Hypothesis: Nonviolent Physical Risk-Taking Enhances Conceptualized Formidability," *Evolution and Human Behavior* 35 (2014): 26–33, doi.org/10.1016/j.evolhumbehav.2013.09.003; Daniel M. T. Fessler, Colin Holbrook, and David Dashoff, "Dressed to Kill? Visible Markers of Coalitional Affiliation Enhance Conceptualized Formidability," *Aggressive Behavior* 42 (2016): 299–309, doi.org/10.1002/ab.21624; Daniel M. T. Fessler, Colin Holbrook, and Matthew M. Gervais, "Men's Physical Strength Moderates Conceptualizations of Prospective Foes in Two Disparate Societies," *Human Nature* 25 (2014): 393–409, doi.org/10.1007/s12110-014-9205-4; Daniel M. T. Fessler, Colin Holbrook, and Jeffrey K. Snyder, "Weapons Make the Man (Larger): Formidability Is Represented as Size and Strength in Humans," *PLOS ONE* 7 (2012): e32751, doi.org/10.1371/journal.pone.0032751; Daniel M. T. Fessler et al., "Sizing Up Helen: Nonviolent Physical Risk-Taking Enhances the Envisioned Bodily Formidability of Women," *Journal of Evolutionary Psychology* 12 (2014): 67–81, doi.org/10.1556/JEP-D-14-00009.

100 We recruited participants: Coltan Scrivner et al., "Gruesomeness Conveys Formidability: Perpetrators of Gratuitously Grisly Acts Are Conceptualized as Larger, Stronger, and More Likely to Win," *Aggressive Behavior* 46, no. 5 (2020): 400–411, doi.org/10.1002/ab.21907.

101 In fact, debates: Marc Alexander, "'The Rigid Embrace of the Narrow House': Premature Burial and the Signs of Death," *Hastings Center Report* 10, no. 3 (1980): 25–31, doi.org/10.2307/3560926.

102 By some estimates: Anthony A. Volk and Jeremy A. Atkinson, "Infant and Child Death in the Human Environment of Evolutionary Adaptation," *Evolution and Human Behavior* 34, no. 3 (2013): 182–92, doi.org/10.1016/j.evolhumbehav .2012.11.007.

102 Anthropologist Clark Barrett: H. Clark Barrett and Tanya Behne, "Children's Understanding of Death as the Cessation of Agency: A Test Using Sleep Versus Death," *Cognition* 96, no. 2 (2004): 93–108, doi.org/10.1016/j.cognition.2004 .05.004.

103 Psychologist Claire White: Claire White, Daniel M. T. Fessler, and Pablo S. Gomez, "The Effects of Corpse Viewing and Corpse Condition on Vigilance for Deceased Loved Ones," *Evolution and Human Behavior* 37, no. 6 (2016): 517–22, doi.org/10.1016/j.evolhumbehav.2016.05.006.

105 In a survey: Claire White, Maya Marin, and Daniel M. T. Fessler, "Not Just Dead Meat: An Evolutionary Account of Corpse Treatment in Mortuary Rituals," *Journal of Cognition and Culture* 17, no. 1–2 (2017): 146–68, doi.org/10.1163 /15685373-12342196.

106 During longer journeys: Caroline Ross, "Park or Ride? Evolution of Infant Carrying in Primates," *International Journal of Primatology* 22, no. 5 (2001): 749–71, doi.org/10.1023/A:1012065332758.

106 As was the case: Volk and Atkinson, "Infant and Child Death in the Human Environment of Evolutionary Adaptation."

107 Infant corpse carrying: Elisa Fernández-Fueyo et al., "Why Do Some Primate Mothers Carry Their Infant's Corpse? A Cross-Species Comparative Study," *Proceedings of the Royal Society B* 288, no. 1959 (2021): 20210590, doi.org/10.1098 /rspb.2021.0590.

107 In a systematic: Fernández-Fueyo et al., "Why Do Some Primate Mothers Carry Their Infant's Corpse?"

108 Disgust evolved as: Megan Oaten, Richard J. Stevenson, and Trevor I. Case, "Disgust as a Disease-Avoidance Mechanism," *Psychological Bulletin* 135, no. 2 (2009): 303–21, doi.org/10.1037/a0014823; Joshua M. Tybur and Debra Lieberman, "Human Pathogen Avoidance Adaptations," *Current Opinion in Psychology* 7 (2016): 6–11, doi.org/10.1016/j.copsyc.2015.06.005; Joshua M. Tybur et al., "Disgust: Evolved Function and Structure," *Psychological Review* 120, no. 1 (2013): 65–84, doi.org/10.1037/a0030778.

109 Just as we have: Mark Schaller and Justin H. Park, "The Behavioral Immune System (and Why It Matters)," *Current Directions in Psychological Science* 20, no. 2 (2011): 99–103, doi.org/10.1177/0963721411402596.

109 Corpses can be pathogenic: World Health Organization, *Risks Posed by Dead Bodies After Disasters* (2013), who.int/publications/m/item/risks-posed-by-dead -bodies-after-disasters.

109 The gagging response: Elisa Becker et al., "The Relationship Between Meat Disgust and Meat Avoidance—a Chicken-and-Egg Problem," *Frontiers in Nutrition* 9 (2022): 958248, doi.org/10.3389/fnut.2022.958248.

109 Unlike scavenging animals: Oksung Chung et al., "The First Whole Genome and Transcriptome of the Cinereous Vulture Reveals Adaptation in the Gastric and Immune Defense Systems and Possible Convergent Evolution Between the Old and New World Vultures," *Genome Biology* 16, no. 215 (2015): Article 215, doi.org/10.1186/s13059-015-0780-4.

109 This theory, which predates: Carl S. Sterner, "A Brief History of Miasmic Theory," *Bulletin of the History of Medicine* 22 (1948): 747–56.

111 Psychologist Tom Kupfer: Tom R. Kupfer, "Why Are Injuries Disgusting? Comparing Pathogen Avoidance and Empathy Accounts," *Emotion* 18, no. 7 (2018): 959–70, doi.org/10.1037/emo0000395.

113 The physiological evidence: Amitai Shenhav and Wendy Berry Mendes, "Aiming for the Stomach and Hitting the Heart: Dissociable Triggers and Sources for Disgust Reactions," *Emotion* 14, no. 2 (2014): 301–9, doi.org/10.1037/a0034644.

114 In my studies: Coltan Scrivner, "The Psychology of Morbid Curiosity: Development and Initial Validation of the Morbid Curiosity Scale," *Personality and Individual Differences* 183 (2021): 111139, doi.org/10.1016/j.paid.2021.111139.

114 Over two thousand years: Plato, *The Republic*, ed. G. R. F. Ferrari, trans. Tom Griffith (Cambridge University Press, 2000), 526a.

CHAPTER SEVEN: THE DEMONS IN OUR DREAMS

118 The historical and: Lydia N. Degarrod, "Coping with Stress: Dream Interpretation in the Mapuche Family," *Psychiatric Journal of the University of Ottawa* 15, no. 2 (1990): 111–16, pubmed.ncbi.nlm.nih.gov/2374787; J. Donald Hughes, "Dream Interpretation in Ancient Civilizations," *Dreaming* 10, no. 1 (2000): 7–18, doi.org/10.1023/a:1009447606158; A. H. M. Kessels, "Ancient Systems of Dream-Classification," *Mnemosyne* 22, no. 4 (1969): 389–424, doi.org/10.1163/156852569x00058; M. J. Meggitt, "Dream Interpretation Among the Mae Enga of New Guinea," *Southwestern Journal of Anthropology* 18, no. 3 (1962): 216–29, doi.org/10.1086/soutjanth.18.3.3628876; Barbara Tedlock, "Zuni and Quiché Dream Sharing and Interpreting," in *Dreaming: Anthropological and Psychological Interpretations*, ed. Barbara Tedlock (Cambridge University Press, 1987).

118 In the Book of: *The Holy Bible* (King James Version) (American Bible Society, 1999): Genesis 37–50.

119 The melody to the Beatles' "Yesterday": Steve Turner, *A Hard Day's Write: The Stories Behind Every Beatles Song* (Carlton Publishing Group, 2010).

119 The structure of the: Malcolm W. Brown, "The Benzene Ring: Dream Analysis," *New York Times*, August 16, 1988, nytimes.com/1988/08/16/science/the-benzene-ring-dream-analysis.html.

120 She dreamt of: Chris Townsend, "Year Without a Summer," *Paris Review*, October 25, 2016, theparisreview.org/blog/2016/10/25/year-without-summer.

120 *Sinister* is a: Jonathan Leggett, "The Scariest Movies—According to Science! 2022 Update," BroadbandChoices, October 5, 2022, broadbandchoices.co.uk/features/science-of-scare.

120 C. Robert Cargill: Jon Lyus, "It Started with a Nightmare: Interview with

Sinister Writer C. Robert Cargill," *HeyUGuys*, October 5, 2012, heyuguys.com/it-started-with-a-dream-interview-sinister-with-writer-c-robert-cargill-exclusive-clip.

120 **When complexity coupled:** George C. Williams, *Adaptation and Natural Selection: A Critique of Some Current Evolutionary Thought* (Princeton University Press, 1966).

121 **Finnish neuroscientist and:** Antti Revonsuo, "The Reinterpretation of Dreams: An Evolutionary Hypothesis of the Function of Dreaming," *Behavioral and Brain Sciences* 23, no. 6 (2000): 877–901, doi.org/10.1017/S0140525X00004015.

121 **It's not easy:** Noor H. Abbas and David R. Samson, "Dreaming During the COVID-19 Pandemic: Support for the Threat Simulation Function of Dreams," *Frontiers in Psychology* 14 (2023), doi.org/10.3389/fpsyg.2023.1124772; Jonas Mathes and Michael Schredl, "Threats in Dreams: Are They Related to Waking-Life?," *International Journal of Dream Research* 9, no. 1 (2016): 58–66, doi.org/10.11588/ijodr.2016.1.27499; Jonas Mathes et al., "The Threat Simulation in Nightmares—Frequency and Characteristics of Dream Threats in Frequent Nightmare Dreamers," *Dreaming* 29, no. 4 (2019): 310–22, doi.org/10.1037/drm0000115; Katja Valli et al., "A Test of the Threat Simulation Theory—Replication of Results in an Independent Sample," *Sleep and Hypnosis* 9, no. 1 (2007): 30–46, psycnet.apa.org/record/2007-13373-005; Katja Valli and Antti Revonsuo, "The Threat Simulation Theory in Light of Recent Empirical Evidence: A Review," *American Journal of Psychology* 122, no. 1 (2009): 17–38, doi.org/10.2307/27784372.

122 **For example, children:** Katja Valli et al., "The Threat Simulation Theory of the Evolutionary Function of Dreaming: Evidence from Dreams of Traumatized Children," *Consciousness and Cognition* 14, no. 1 (2003): 188–218, doi.org/10.1016/s1053-8100(03)00019-9.

122 **Increased daily stress:** Odalis Garcia et al., "What Goes Around Comes Around: Nightmares and Daily Stress Are Bidirectionally Associated in Nurses," *Stress and Health* 37, no. 5 (2021): 1035–42, doi.org/10.1002/smi.3048; Michael Schredl, "Effects of State and Trait Factors on Nightmare Frequency," *European Archives of Psychiatry and Clinical Neuroscience* 253, no. 5 (2003): 241–47, doi.org/10.1007/s00406-003-0438-1; Michael Schredl et al., "Nightmares and Stress: A Longitudinal Study," *Journal of Clinical Sleep Medicine* 15, no. 09 (2019): 1209–15, doi.org/10.5664/jcsm.7904.

122 **Relatedly, people who:** Martina Köthe and Reinhard Pietrowsky, "Behavioral Effects of Nightmares and Their Correlations to Personality Patterns," *Dreaming* 11, no. 1 (2001): 43–52, doi.org/10.1023/a:1009468517557; Barry Krakow et al., "Nightmare Frequency in Sexual Assault Survivors with PTSD," *Journal of Anxiety Disorders* 16, no. 2 (2002): 175–90, doi.org/10.1016/s0887-6185(02)00093-2; Tammy T. Nguyen et al., "Nightmare Frequency, Nightmare Distress, and Anxiety," *Perceptual and Motor Skills* 95, no. 1 (2002): 219–25, doi.org/10.2466/pms.2002.95.1.219.

123 **Anthropologist Thomas Gregor:** Thomas Gregor, "A Content Analysis of Mehinaku Dreams," *Ethos* 9, no. 4 (1981): 353–90, doi.org/10.1525/eth.1981.9.4.02a00070.

125 **His research shows:** David R. Samson et al., "Evidence for an Emotional Adaptive Function of Dreams: A Cross-Cultural Study," *Scientific Reports* 13, no. 1 (2023), doi.org/10.1038/s41598-023-43319-z.

126 **For example, humans:** Richard G. Coss, "The Ethological Command in Art," *Leonardo* 1, no. 3 (1968): 273, doi.org/10.2307/1571871; James G. Hamilton, "Needle Phobia: A Neglected Diagnosis," *Journal of Family Practice* 41, no. 2 (1995): 169–75, pubmed.ncbi.nlm.nih.gov/7636457.

126 **We have evolved a predisposition:** Steven Pinker, *The Language Instinct: How the Mind Creates Language* (Penguin UK, 2003).

127 **Novelty itself is:** Daniel Ernst, Stefanie Becker, and Gernot Horstmann, "Novelty Competes with Saliency for Attention," *Vision Research* 168 (2020): 42–52, doi.org/10.1016/j.visres.2020.01.004.

127 **The early months:** Eirin Fränkl et al., "How Our Dreams Changed During the COVID-19 Pandemic: Effects and Correlates of Dream Recall Frequency—a Multinational Study on 19,355 Adults," *Nature and Science of Sleep* 13 (2021): 1573–91, doi.org/10.2147/nss.s324142; Maurizio Gorgoni, Serena Scarpelli, Valentina Alfonsi, and Luigi De Gennaro, "Dreaming During the COVID-19 Pandemic: A Narrative Review," *Neuroscience & Biobehavioral Reviews* 138 (2022): 104710, doi.org/10.1016/j.neubiorev.2022.104710; Anu-Katriina Pesonen et al., "Pandemic Dreams: Network Analysis of Dream Content During the COVID-19 Lockdown," *Frontiers in Psychology* 11 (2020), doi.org/10.3389/fpsyg.2020.573961; Serena Scarpelli et al., "Pandemic Nightmares: Effects on Dream Activity of the COVID-19 Lockdown in Italy," *Journal of Sleep Research* 30, no. 5 (2021), doi.org/10.1111/jsr.13300; Michael Schredl and Kelly Bulkeley, "Dreaming and the COVID-19 Pandemic: A Survey in a US Sample," *Dreaming* 30, no. 3 (2020): 189, doi.org/10.1037/drm0000146.

127 **Those who were more:** Kathryn E. R. Kennedy et al., "Nightmare Content During the COVID-19 Pandemic: Influence of COVID-Related Stress and Sleep Disruption in the United States," *Journal of Sleep Research* 31, no. 1 (2021), doi.org/10.1111/jsr.13439.

128 **In many animals, the:** Drew B. Headley et al., "Embracing Complexity in Defensive Networks," *Neuron* 103, no. 2 (2019): 189–201, doi.org/10.1016/j.neuron.2019.05.024; Alex Tendler and Shlomo Wagner, "Different Types of Theta Rhythmicity Are Induced by Social and Fearful Stimuli in a Network Associated with Social Memory," *eLife* 4 (2015), doi.org/10.7554/elife.03614.

128 **Interestingly, the hippocampal:** Akihiro Karashima et al., "Instantaneous Acceleration and Amplification of Hippocampal Theta Wave Coincident with Phasic Pontine Activities During REM Sleep," *Brain Research* 1051, no. 1–2 (2005): 50–56, doi.org/10.1016/j.brainres.2005.05.055.

128 **Because REM sleep:** Joshua Feriante and John F. Arujo, "Physiology, REM

Sleep," in *StatPearls* (StatPearls Publishing, 2023), ncbi.nlm.nih.gov/books/NBK 531454.

130 **For example, one group:** Jean-Pierre Sastre and Michel Jouvet, "The Oneiric Behavior of the Cat," *Physiology & Behavior* 22 no. 5 (1979): 979–89, psycnet.apa .org/record/1980-27526-001.

131 **Incredibly, the researchers:** H. Freyja Ólafsdóttir et al., "Hippocampal Place Cells Construct Reward Related Sequences Through Unexplored Space," *eLife* 4 (2015), doi.org/10.7554/elife.06063.

132 **The last common:** Nikolaus Rajewsky, "Octopus Intelligence Sheds Light on Evolution of Complex Brains," *Genetic Engineering & Biotechnology News*, December 29, 2022, genengnews.com/topics/omics/octopus-intelligence-sheds-light-on -evolution-of-complex-brains.

132 **During active sleep:** Aditi Pophale et al., "Wake-Like Skin Patterning and Neural Activity During Octopus Sleep," *Nature* 619, no. 7968 (2023): 129–34, doi.org/10.1038/s41586-023-06203-4.

132 **Occasionally, the octopus:** Eric A. Ramos et al., "Abnormal Behavioral Episodes Associated with Sleep and Quiescence in *Octopus insularis*: Possible Nightmares in a Cephalopod?" bioRxiv (2023), doi.org/10.1101/2023.05.11.540348.

CHAPTER EIGHT: THE DARK EMPATH

136 **When I looked:** Cynthia A. Hoffner and Kenneth J. Levine, "Enjoyment of Mediated Fright and Violence: A Meta-Analysis," *Media Psychology* 7, no. 2 (2005): 207–37, doi.org/10.1207/s1532785xmep0702_5.

140 **However, the data:** Coltan Scrivner, "Bleeding-Heart Horror Fans: Enjoyment of Horror Media Is Not Related to Lower Empathy or Compassion," *Journal of Media Psychology* 36, no. 1 (2024), https://econtent.hogrefe.com/doi/10.1027/1864 -1105/a000405.

141 **"In every passion":** Adam Smith, *The Theory of Moral Sentiments* (Penguin, 2010).

141 **Modern scientific takes:** Jean Decety and Philip L. Jackson, "A Social-Neuroscience Perspective on Empathy," *Current Directions in Psychological Science* 15, no. 2 (2006): 54–58, doi.org/10.1111/j.0963-7214.2006.00406.x; Jamil Zaki and Kevin N. Ochsner, "The Neuroscience of Empathy: Progress, Pitfalls and Promise," *Nature Neuroscience* 15, no. 5 (2012): 675–80, doi.org/10.1038/nn.3085.

141 **Cognitive empathy corresponds:** Shannon Spaulding, "Cognitive Empathy," in *The Routledge Handbook of Philosophy of Empathy*, ed. Heidi L. Maibom (Routledge, 2017); Marcello Spinella, "Prefrontal Substrates of Empathy: Psychometric Evidence in a Community Sample," *Biological Psychology* 70, no. 3 (2005): 175–81, doi.org/10.1016/j.biopsycho.2004.01.005.

141 **Affective empathy is:** Heidi L. Maibom, "Affective Empathy," in *The Routledge Handbook of Philosophy of Empathy*, ed. Heidi L. Maibom (Routledge, 2017).

142 **Mathias Clasen gives:** Mathias Clasen, *A Very Nervous Person's Guide to Horror Movies* (Oxford University Press, 2021).

143 **Still, there's a mound:** Chris D. Frith and Uta Frith, "The Neural Basis of Mentalizing," *Neuron* 50, no. 4 (2006): 531–34, doi.org/10.1016/j.neuron.2006.05.001; Lauri Nummenmaa et al., "Is Emotional Contagion Special? An fMRI Study on Neural Systems for Affective and Cognitive Empathy," *NeuroImage* 43, no. 3 (2008): 571–80, doi.org/10.1016/j.neuroimage.2008.08.014; Carme Uribe et al., "Neuroanatomical and Functional Correlates of Cognitive and Affective Empathy in Young Healthy Adults," *Frontiers in Behavioral Neuroscience* 13 (2019), doi .org/10.3389/fnbeh.2019.00085.

143 **The aptly named:** Renate L. E. P. Reniers et al., "The QCAE: A Questionnaire of Cognitive and Affective Empathy," *Journal of Personality Assessment* 93, no. 1 (2010): 84–95, doi.org/10.1080/00223891.2010.528484.

144 **It measures different:** Scott O. Lilienfeld and Michelle R. Widows, *Psychopathic Personality Inventory–Revised: Professional Manual* (Psychological Assessment Resources, 2005); Katarzyna Uzieblo et al., "The Validity of the Psychopathic Personality Inventory–Revised in a Community Sample," *Assessment* 17, no. 3 (2009): 334–46, doi.org/10.1177/1073191109356544.

145 **For my purposes:** Rotten Tomatoes Editorial Staff, "Slashers and Monsters and Gore, Oh My! Which Horror Subgenre Is the Best?" *Rotten Tomatoes*, June 3, 2021, editorial.rottentomatoes.com/article/slashers-and-monsters-and-gore-oh-my -which-horror-subgenre-is-the-best.

146 **Replicating my previous:** Scrivner, "Bleeding-Heart Horror Fans."

147 **In economics and:** Colin Camerer and Richard H. Thaler, "Anomalies: Ultimatums, Dictators and Manners," *Journal of Economic Perspectives* 9, no. 2 (1995): 209–19, doi.org/10.1257/jep.9.2.209; Francesco Guala and Luigi Mittone, "Paradigmatic Experiments: The Dictator Game," *Journal of Socio-Economics* 39, no. 5 (2009): 578–84, doi.org/10.1016/j.socec.2009.05.007.

149 **As a result, many:** Stanley Milgram, "Behavioral Study of Obedience," *Journal of Abnormal & Social Psychology* 67, no. 4 (1963): 371–78, doi.org/10.1037/h0040525; Craig Haney, Curtis Banks, and Philip Zimbardo, "A Study of Prisoners and Guards in a Simulated Prison," *Naval Research Reviews* 30, no. 9 (1973): 4–17, simplypsychology.org/wp-content/uploads/zimbardo-paper.pdf.

149 **In a now hugely:** Delroy L. Paulhus and Kevin M. Williams, "The Dark Triad of Personality: Narcissism, Machiavellianism, and Psychopathy," *Journal of Research in Personality* 36, no. 6 (2002): 556–63, doi.org/10.1016/s0092-6566(02)00505-6.

149 **The word "narcissism":** Mark Cartwright, "Narcissus," *World History Encyclopedia*, last modified March 5, 2023, worldhistory.org/Narcissus.

150 **Psychologists have identified:** Kelly A. Dickinson and Aaron L. Pincus, "Interpersonal Analysis of Grandiose and Vulnerable Narcissism," *Journal of Personality Disorders* 17, no. 3 (2003): 188–207, doi.org/10.1521/pedi.17.3.188 .22146; Joshua D. Miller et al., "Grandiose and Vulnerable Narcissism: A Nomological Network Analysis," *Journal of Personality* 79, no. 5 (2010): 1013–42, doi .org/10.1111/j.1467-6494.2010.00711.x; Javier I. Borráz-León et al., "Cortisol Reactivity to Psychosocial Stress in Vulnerable and Grandiose Narcissists: An

Exploratory Study," *Frontiers in Psychology* 13 (2023), doi.org/10.3389/fpsyg.2022 .1067456.

150 **The term "Machiavellianism":** Daniel N. Jones and Delroy L. Paulhus, "Machiavellianism," in *Handbook of Individual Differences in Social Behavior*, ed. Mark R. Leary and Rick H. Hoyle (Guilford Press, 2009).

151 **Subclinical psychopathy, which:** James M. LeBreton, John F. Binning, and Anthony J. Adorno, "Subclinical Psychopaths," in *Comprehensive Handbook of Personality and Psychopathology*, vol. 1, ed. Jay C. Thomas and Daniel L. Segal (John Wiley & Sons, 2006).

151 **Those high in subclinical:** Scott O. Lilienfeld and Brian P. Andrews, "Development and Preliminary Validation of a Self-Report Measure of Psychopathic Personality Traits in Noncriminal Population," *Journal of Personality Assessment* 66, no. 3 (1996): 488–524, doi.org/10.1207/s15327752jpa6603_3.

152 **A few years ago:** Nadja Heym et al., "The Dark Empath: Characterising Dark Traits in the Presence of Empathy," *Personality and Individual Differences* 169 (2020): 110172, doi.org/10.1016/j.paid.2020.110172.

152 **According to years:** Peter K. Jonason and Laura Krause, "The Emotional Deficits Associated with the Dark Triad Traits: Cognitive Empathy, Affective Empathy, and Alexithymia," *Personality and Individual Differences* 55, no. 5 (2013): 532–37, doi.org/10.1016/j.paid.2013.04.027.

154 **Some researchers have:** Daniel Nelson Jones and Aurelio Jose Figueredo, "The Core of Darkness: Uncovering the Heart of the Dark Triad," *European Journal of Personality* 27, no. 6 (2012): 521–31, doi.org/10.1002/per.1893.

154 **It might not:** Petri J. Kajonius and Therese Björkman, "Individuals with Dark Traits Have the Ability but Not the Disposition to Empathize," *Personality and Individual Differences* 155 (2019): 109716, doi.org/10.1016/j.paid.2019.109716.

155 **In his book:** Simon Baron-Cohen, *The Science of Evil: On Empathy and the Origins of Cruelty* (Basic Books, 2011).

155 **Psychologist Paul Bloom:** Paul Bloom, *Against Empathy: The Case for Rational Compassion* (HarperCollins, 2017).

156 **Focusing on a single:** Tehila Kogut and Ilana Ritov, "The Singularity Effect of Identified Victims in Separate and Joint Evaluations," *Organizational Behavior and Human Decision Processes* 97, no. 2 (2005): 106–16, doi.org/10.1016/j.obhdp .2005.02.003.

156 **This leads us:** C. Daniel Batson, Tricia R. Klein, Lori Highberger, and Laura L. Shaw, "Immorality from Empathy-Induced Altruism: When Compassion and Justice Conflict," *Journal of Personality and Social Psychology* 68, no. 6 (1995): 1042–54, doi.org/10.1037/0022-3514.68.6.1042; Paul Bloom, "Empathy and Its Discontents," *Trends in Cognitive Sciences* 21, no. 1 (2017): 24–31, doi.org/10.1016 /j.tics.2016.11.004.

158 **This brings us:** Hwan Kim and Sumi Han, "Does Personal Distress Enhance Empathic Interaction or Block It?," *Personality and Individual Differences* 124 (2017): 77–83, doi.org/10.1016/j.paid.2017.12.005; Helen Wilkinson, Richard Whittington, Laura Perry, and Catrin Eames, "Examining the Relationship Be-

tween Burnout and Empathy in Healthcare Professionals: A Systematic Review," *Burnout Research* 6 (2017): 18–29, doi.org/10.1016/j.burn.2017.06.003.

159 Rather than building: Bloom, *Against Empathy*.

CHAPTER NINE: SCARY MOVIES IN SCARY TIMES

162 By the first week: Nicole Sperling, "'Contagion,' Steven Soderbergh's 2011 Thriller, Is Climbing Up the Charts," *New York Times*, March 4, 2020, nytimes .com/2020/03/04/business/media/coronavirus-contagion-movie.html.

163 This pandemic was: Heidi Hagemann, "The 1918 Flu Pandemic Was Brutal, Killing More Than 50 Million People Worldwide," aired April 2, 2020, on NPR, npr.org/2020/04/02/826358104/the-1918-flu-pandemic-was-brutal-killing -as-many-as-100-million-people-worldwide; David M. Morens, Jeffery K. Tauben- berger, and Anthony S. Fauci, "The Persistent Legacy of the 1918 Influenza Virus," *New England Journal of Medicine* 361, no. 3 (2009): 225–29, doi.org/10.1056 /nejmp0904819.

166 My morbidly curious: Coltan Scrivner, "An Infectious Curiosity: Morbid Curi- osity and Media Preferences During a Pandemic," *Evolutionary Studies in Imagi- native Culture* 5, no. 1 (2021): 1–12, doi.org/10.26613/esic.5.1.206.

168 This didn't seem: Nash Information Services, "Box Office History for Horror," The Numbers, August 2, 2023, the-numbers.com/market/genre/Horror.

170 The scale consists: Coltan Scrivner, John A. Johnson, Jens Kjeldgaard- Christiansen, and Mathias Clasen, "Pandemic Practice: Horror Fans and Morbidly Curious Individuals Are More Psychologically Resilient during the COVID-19 Pandemic," *Personality and Individual Differences* 168 (2021): 110397, doi.org/10 .1016/j.paid.2020.110397.

172 These five traits: Oliver P. John and Sanjay Srivastava, "The Big-Five Trait Tax- onomy: History, Measurement, and Theoretical Perspectives," in *Handbook of Personality: Theory and Research*, vol. 2, ed. Lawrence A. Pervin and Oliver P. John (Guilford Press, 1999).

172 As we predicted: Coltan Scrivner et al., "Pandemic Practice: Horror Fans and Morbidly Curious Individuals Are More Psychologically Resilient During the COVID-19 Pandemic," *Personality and Individual Differences* 168 (2020): 110397, doi.org/10.1016/j.paid.2020.110397.

173 While the strongest: Coltan Scrivner, "The Psychology of Morbid Curiosity: De- velopment and Initial Validation of the Morbid Curiosity Scale," *Personality and Individual Differences* 183 (2021): 111139, doi.org/10.1016/j.paid.2021.111139.

174 Back in the early 2000s: Yuliya Strizhakova and Marina Krcmar, "Mood Man- agement and Video Rental Choices," *Media Psychology* 10, no. 1 (2007): 91–112, tandfonline.com/doi/abs/10.1080/15213260701301152.

175 This makes intuitive: Dolf Zillmann, "Mood Management in the Context of Selective Exposure Theory," *Annals of the International Communication Association* 23, no. 1 (2000): 103–23, doi.org/10.1080/23808985.2000.11678971.

175 A group of researchers: Gideon Nave, Jason Rentfrow, and Sudeep Bhatia, "We

Are What We Watch: Movie Plots Predict the Personalities of Their Fans," PsyArXiv Preprints (2020), https://doi.org/10.31234/osf.io/wsdu8

CHAPTER TEN: TERRIFYING THERAPY

179 Humans are drawn: Yair Bar-Haim et al., "Threat-Related Attentional Bias in Anxious and Nonanxious Individuals: A Meta-Analytic Study," *Psychological Bulletin* 133, no. 1 (2007): 1–24, doi.org/10.1037/0033-2909.133.1.1.

179 Anxiety evolved because: Melissa Bateson, Ben Brilot, and Daniel Nettle, "Anxiety: An Evolutionary Approach," *Canadian Journal of Psychiatry* 56, no. 12 (2011): 707–15, doi.org/10.1177/070674371105601202; Tara A. Karasewich and Valerie A. Kuhlmeier, "Trait Social Anxiety as a Conditional Adaptation: A Developmental and Evolutionary Framework," *Developmental Review* 55 (2020): 100886, doi.org /10.1016/j.dr.2019.100886; Isaac M. Marks and Randolph M. Nesse, "Fear and Fitness: An Evolutionary Analysis of Anxiety Disorders," *Ethology and Sociobiology* 15, no. 5–6 (1994): 247–61, doi.org/10.1016/0162-3095(94)90002-7.

180 For example, people: Stéphane Bouchard et al., "Anxiety Increases the Feeling of Presence in Virtual Reality," *PRESENCE: Virtual and Augmented Reality* 17, no. 4 (2008): 376–91, doi.org/10.1162/pres.17.4.376.

180 Similarly, individuals with: Yun Ling et al., "A Meta-Analysis on the Relationship Between Self-Reported Presence and Anxiety in Virtual Reality Exposure Therapy for Anxiety Disorders," *PLOS ONE* 9, no. 5 (2014): e96144, doi.org/10 .1371/journal.pone.0096144.

181 Horror movies can: Coltan Scrivner, "Scaring Away Anxiety: Therapeutic Avenues for Horror Fiction to Enhance Treatment for Anxiety Symptoms," PsyArXiv Preprints (2021), doi.org/10.31234/osf.io/7uh6f.

181 There can be stigma: Christopher Curcio and Denise Corboy, "Stigma and Anxiety Disorders: A Systematic Review," *Stigma and Health* 5, no. 2 (2019): 125–37, doi.org/10.1037/sah0000183.

181 Suppression can sometimes: Tammy English and Oliver P. John, "Understanding the Social Effects of Emotion Regulation: The Mediating Role of Authenticity for Individual Differences in Suppression," *Emotion* 13, no. 2 (2012): 314–29, doi.org/10.1037/a0029847.

185 They also found: Margee Kerr, Greg J. Siegle, and Jahala Orsini, "Voluntary Arousing Negative Experiences (VANE): Why We Like to Be Scared," *Emotion* 19, no. 4 (2018): 682–98, doi.org/10.1037/emo0000470.

187 Exposure therapy has been: American Psychological Association, Presidential Task Force on Evidence-Based Practice, "Evidence-Based Practice in Psychology," *American Psychologist* 61, no. 4 (2006): 271–85, doi.org/10.1037/0003-066X.61 .4.271.

187 Exposure therapy decreases: Friederike Raeder et al., "The Association Between Fear Extinction, the Ability to Accomplish Exposure and Exposure Therapy Outcome in Specific Phobia," *Scientific Reports* 10, no. 1 (2020), doi.org/10 .1038/s41598-020-61004-3.

188 **The great thing:** Hannah Boettcher, C. Alex Brake, and David H. Barlow, "Origins and Outlook of Interoceptive Exposure," *Journal of Behavior Therapy and Experimental Psychiatry* 53 (2016): 41–51, doi.org/10.1016/j.jbtep.2015.10.009.

190 **He and his team:** Mathias Clasen, Marc Andersen, and Uffe Schjoedt, "Adrenaline Junkies and White-Knucklers: A Quantitative Study of Fear Management in Haunted House Visitors," *Poetics* 73 (2019): 61–71, doi.org/10.1016/j.poetic .2019.01.002.

193 **Our data from the haunt:** Marc Malmdorf Andersen et al., "Playing with Fear: A Field Study in Recreational Horror," *Psychological Science* 31, no. 12 (2020): 1497–510, doi.org/10.1177/0956797620972116.

195 **Horror dexterously tugs:** Lauri Nummenmaa, "Psychology and Neurobiology of Horror Movies," PsyArXiv Preprints (2021), doi.org/10.31234/osf.io/b8tgs.

195 **Several psychological studies:** Ron Tamborini and James Stiff, "Predictors of Horror Film Attendance and Appeal: An Analysis of the Audience for Frightening Films," *Communication Research* 14, no. 4 (1987): 415–36, doi.org/10.1177/00936 5087014004003; Emily D. Edwards, "The Relationship Between Sensation-Seeking and Horror Movie Interest and Attendance" (PhD diss., University of Tennessee, 1984); Marvin Zuckerman and Patrick Litle, "Personality and Curiosity About Morbid and Sexual Events," *Personality and Individual Differences* 7, no. 1 (1986): 49–56, doi.org/10.1016/0191-8869(86)90107-8.

197 **I took dozens:** Coltan Scrivner et al., "The Psychological Benefits of Scary Play in Three Types of Horror Fans," *Journal of Media Psychology* 35, no. 2 (2022): 87–98, doi.org/10.1027/1864-1105/a000354.

201 **Play evolved because:** Peter K. Smith, "Does Play Matter? Functional and Evolutionary Aspects of Animal and Human Play," *Behavioral and Brain Sciences* 5, no. 1 (1982): 139–55, doi.org/10.1017/s0140525x0001092x; Francis Steen and Stephanie Owens, "Evolution's Pedagogy: An Adaptationist Model of Pretense and Entertainment," *Journal of Cognition and Culture* 1, no. 4 (2001): 289–321, doi.org/10.1163/156853701753678305.

CHAPTER ELEVEN: THE KIDS ARE ALL SPOOKY

205 **Humans have an unusually:** Barry Bogin, "The Evolution of Human Childhood," *BioScience* 40, no. 1 (1990): 16–25, doi.org/10.2307/1311235; John Bock and Daniel W. Sellen, "Childhood and the Evolution of the Human Life Course: An Introduction," *Human Nature* 13, no. 2 (2002): 153–59, doi.org/10.1007/s12110-002 -1006-5; Tanya M. Smith et al., "Dental Evidence for Ontogenetic Differences Between Modern Humans and Neanderthals," *Proceedings of the National Academy of Sciences* 107, no. 49 (2010): 20923–28, doi.org/10.1073/pnas.1010906107.

205 **Rather than transition:** Barry Bogin, "Modern Human Life History: The Evolution of Human Childhood and Fertility," in *The Evolution of Human Life History*, ed. Kristen Hawkes and Richard R. Paine (School of American Research Press, 2006).

205 **Whereas our chimpanzee cousins:** Jennifer L. Thompson and Andrew J. Nelson,

"Middle Childhood and Modern Human Origins," *Human Nature* 22, no. 3 (2011): 249–80, doi.org/10.1007/s12110-011-9119-3.

206 The current estimate: Anthony A. Volk and Jeremy A. Atkinson, "Infant and Child Death in the Human Environment of Evolutionary Adaptation," *Evolution and Human Behavior* 34, no. 3 (2013): 182–92, doi.org/10.1016/j.evolhumbehav.2012.11.007.

207 Psychologist Alison Gopnik: Alison Gopnik, "Childhood as a Solution to Explore–Exploit Tensions," *Philosophical Transactions of the Royal Society B* 375, no. 1803 (2020): 20190502, doi.org/10.1098/rstb.2019.0502.

207 In adults, the brain: Christopher W. Kuzawa et al., "Metabolic Costs and Evolutionary Implications of Human Brain Development," *Proceedings of the National Academy of Sciences* 111, no. 36 (2014): 13010–15, doi.org/10.1073/pnas.1323099111.

208 Frequency and complexity: Sandra Aamodt and Sam Wang, *Welcome to Your Child's Brain: How the Mind Grows from Birth to University* (Simon & Schuster, 2011).

209 It's no surprise: Owen Aldis, *Play-Fighting* (Academic Press, 1975); S. L. Hall, "Object Play by Adult Animals," in *Animal Play: Evolutionary, Comparative, and Ecological Perspectives*, ed. Marc Bekoff and John A. Byers (Cambridge University Press, 1998).

210 Humans arguably have: Caroline Schuppli et al., "Life History, Cognition and the Evolution of Complex Foraging Niches," *Journal of Human Evolution* 92 (2016): 91–100, doi.org/10.1016/j.jhevol.2015.11.007.

211 They found that songs: Marc Malmdorf Andersen et al., "Titte-bøh! Frygt og leg i danske daginstitutioner," *Dansk Pædagogisk Tidsskrift* (2022), dpt.dk/teman umre/2022-1/titte-boeh-frygt-og-leg-i-danske-daginstitutioner.

212 One of the most influential: Peter Gray, "Evolutionary Functions of Play: Practice, Resilience, Innovation, and Cooperation," in *The Cambridge Handbook of Play: Developmental and Disciplinary Perspectives*, ed. P. K. Smith and J. L. Roopnarine (Cambridge University Press, 2018), doi.org/10.1017/9781108131384.006; Marek Spinka, Ruth C. Newberry, and Marc Bekoff, "Mammalian Play: Training for the Unexpected," *Quarterly Review of Biology* 76, no. 2 (2001): 141–68, doi.org/10.1086/393866.

216 For example, one randomized: Tiffany Y. L. Tsui et al., "Reductions of Anxiety Symptoms, State Anxiety, and Anxious Arousal in Youth Playing the Videogame MindLight Compared to Online Cognitive Behavioral Therapy," *Games for Health Journal* (2021), doi.org/10.1089/g4h.2020.0083.

216 Another study found: Aniek Wols et al., "In-Game Play Behaviours During an Applied Video Game for Anxiety Prevention Predict Successful Intervention Outcomes," *Journal of Psychopathology and Behavioral Assessment* 40, no. 4 (2018): 655–68, doi.org/10.1007/s10862-018-9684-4.

218 In 2015, a Maryland couple: Donna St. George, "Parents Investigated for Neglect After Letting Kids Walk Home Alone," *Washington Post*, January 14, 2015, washingtonpost.com/local/education/maryland-couple-want-free-range-kids

-but-not-all-do/2015/01/14/d406c0be-9c0f-11e4-bcfb-059ec7a93ddc_story
.html.

219 Climbing trees, jumping: Helen F. Dodd and Kathryn J. Lester, "Adventurous
Play as a Mechanism for Reducing Risk for Childhood Anxiety: A Conceptual
Model," *Clinical Child and Family Psychology Review* 24, no. 1 (2021): 164–81,
doi.org/10.1007/s10567-020-00338-w.

219 As children confront: Ellen Beate Hansen Sandseter and Leif Edward Ottesen
Kennair, "Children's Risky Play from an Evolutionary Perspective: The Anti-
Phobic Effects of Thrilling Experiences," *Evolutionary Psychology* 9, no. 2 (2011),
doi.org/10.1177/147470491100900212.

219 As unsupervised, thrilling: Peter Gray, "The Decline of Play and the Rise of
Psychopathology in Children and Adolescents," *American Journal of Play* 3, no. 4
(2011): 443–63, files.eric.ed.gov/fulltext/EJ985541.pdf.

CHAPTER TWELVE: A MISUNDERSTOOD VIRTUE

221 The first was: Lionel Dahmer, *A Father's Story* (Echo Point Books, 2021).

222 The second odd: Peter Vronsky, *American Serial Killers: The Epidemic Years 1950–
2000* (Berkley, 2021).

222 At one point, Dahmer: *Conversations with a Killer: The Jeffrey Dahmer Tapes*,
season 1, episode 2, "Can I Take Your Picture?," directed by Joe Berlinger, aired
October 7, 2022, on Netflix.

223 One of the rumors: Patrick M. Markey and Christopher J. Ferguson, *Moral
Combat: Why the War on Violent Video Games Is Wrong* (BenBella Books, 2017).

224 He himself claimed: *Inside Edition*, "Inside the Mind of Jeffrey Dahmer: Serial
Killer's Chilling Jailhouse Interview," aired 1993, insideedition.com/media
/videos/inside-mind-jeffrey-dahmer-serial-killers-chilling-jailhouse-interview
-48748.

225 About 20 percent of school: Markey and Ferguson, *Moral Combat*.

226 It's clear from: Margaret L. Kern et al., "Social Media–Predicted Personality Traits
and Values Can Help Match People to Their Ideal Jobs," *Proceedings of the National
Academy of Sciences* 116, no. 52 (2019): 26459–64, doi.org/10.1073/pnas.1917942116;
John W. Lounsbury et al., "An Investigation of the Personality Traits of Scientists
Versus Nonscientists and Their Relationship with Career Satisfaction," *R&D Management* 42, no. 1 (2011): 47–59, doi.org/10.1111/j.1467-9310.2011.00665.x; Tobias
Wolfram, "(Not Just) Intelligence Stratifies the Occupational Hierarchy: Ranking
360 Professions by IQ and Non-Cognitive Traits," *Intelligence* 98 (2023): 101755,
doi.org/10.1016/j.intell.2023.101755.

227 Funeral workers also: Andrew F. A. Arena et al., "Living Authentically in the
Face of Death: Predictors of Autonomous Motivation Among Individuals Exposed to Chronic Mortality Cues Compared to a Matched Community Sample,"
OMEGA—Journal of Death and Dying 89, no. 1 (2022): 379–403, doi.org/10
.1177/00302228221074160.

INDEX

Page numbers in italics indicate photographs.